Keeter & Sinquefield's
Habeas Citebook:

How to Overcome
Prosecutorial Misconduct

Written by:
Jackie R. Keeter
&
Kevin Sinquefield

CP

Cadmus Publishing
www.cadmuspublishing.com

FOREWORD
FROM THE AUTHORS

For the last 20 years, I have been fighting and winning cases on every issue that can be raised on a writ of habeas corpus for Texas prisoners. The last few years, the justice system has become more and more aware of prosecutors that bend the rules of fairness to win at all cost, even to the point of convicting innocent people. Prosecutorial misconduct has reached epidemic proportions in recent years, and the Federal and State Reporters bear testimony to this unsettling trend. Just turn the pages of this book, when a public official behaves with such disregard for his constitutional obligations and the rights of the accused, it erodes the public trust in our justice system, and chips away at the foundational premises of the rule of law.

When such transgressions are acknowledged yet forgiven by the courts, it does nothing, but invites their repetitions. Prosecutorial misconduct has become a thorn in the side of the justice system for the past several years. over 80 years ago the United States Supreme Court rang the bell on the duties of a prosecutor in Berger-V-United States, 292 U.S. 78, 88, 55 S.CT. 629, 633, 79 L.ED. 1314 (1935) (The United States Attorney is the representative not of an ordinary party to a controversy, but of a sovereignty whose obligation to govern impartially is as compelling as its obligation to govern at all, and whose interest, therefore, in a criminal prosecution is not that it shall win a case, but that justice shall be done. As such he is in a peculiar and very definite sentence the servant of the law, the twofold aim of which is that guilt shall not escape or innocence suffer. He may prosecute with earnestness and vigor-indeed, he should do so. But, while he may strike hard blows, he is not at liberty to strike fowl ones, it is as much his duty to refrain from improper methods calculated to produce a wrongful conviction as it is to use every legitimate means to bring about a just one).

In Berger the United States Supreme Court made it very clear, as to what the duties of a prosecutor were. This cite book will assist you in finding favorable case law based on almost any subject that relates to prosecutor misconduct. In light of the 1996 Anti-terrorism and effective death penalty act, it is extremely difficult to obtain relief on your 28 U.S.C. §§ 2254 or 225 writs.

Under the AEDPA, standard of review, Federal Courts cannot grant habeas corpus relief in connection with any claim that was adjudicated on the merits in State or Federal Court proceedings, unless the adjudication of that claim either: (1) resulted in a decision that was contrary to, or involved an unreasonable application of clearly established law, as determined by the Supreme Court of the United States, or (2) resulted in a decision that was based on an unreasonable determination of the facts in light of the evidence presented in State or Federal District Court proceedings. See <u>Brown-V-Payton</u>, 544 U.S. 133, 141, 125 S.CT. 1432, 1438, 161 L.ED.2d 334 (2005); <u>Williams-V-Taylor</u>, 529 U.S. 362, 404-405, 120 S.CT. 1495, 1519, 146 L.ED.2d (2000); 28 U.S.C. §§ 2254(d)(l)(2) & 2255. This book will help anyone preparing a writ in State or Federal Court. The Authors also suggest, that before using any of the cases cited herein, to check and make sure they are still good law.

JACKIE R. KEETER & KEVIN SINQUEFIELD

DEDICATIONS & ACKNOWLEDGMENTS:

This book is dedicated to all the men and women, held in prisons within the United States and other countries, that are either innocent or was denied a fair trial at the hands of a corrupt prosecutor. I hope that this book helps you in your fight for justice, and your freedom. Remember "NEVER GIVE UP"!!!!!

We would also like to thank Juan Gonzales, for helping design the original cover for the book, although we never used it. I would like to thank the law library clerks for all of their hard work, in making sure we had the cases we needed to complete this book after three long years of hard work.

ABOUT THE AUTHORS:

Jackie R. Keeter, is the lead author of Keeter and Sinquefield's habeas cite book, how to overcome prosecutor misconduct. For the past 20 plus years, Mr. Keeter has been fighting to obtain justice for inmates, within the Texas Department of Criminal Justice. In that time, he has had some very impressive wins, which gained some new trials. Mr. Keeter is a graduate of the Black Stone Paralegal college, and is also a member of the National Lawyers Guild.

Mr. Sinquefield, is an up-and-coming Paralegal. He is a Graduate of the Black Stone Paralegal Institute. He is a great legal research expert as well as a litigator. He plans on opening his own paralegal service someday.

PREPARING FOR POST CONVICTION RELIEF IN FEDERAL COURT:

The following are a list of basic documents that you will need in order to file your writ in the Federal Court system. These documents, include both State and Federal investigative agencies.

<u>DOCUMENTS NEEDED TO CONTEST A GUILTY PLEA:</u>

1. Police reports, DEA 5 to 6 reports, FBI reports, ATF reports;
2. Indictment or Information;
3. Docket Entry Sheet along with all Motions filed;
4. Motion to Suppress, Search Warrant, Arrest Warrant, Affidavits whatever was used to obtain the search warrant;
5. Suppression hearing transcripts (if any held);
6. Guilty plea transcripts;
7. Letters from attorney advising prisoner to plead guilty or what the terms of your plea agreement is if you have any;
8. PSI Reports (if any);
9. Objection to PSI Reports;
10. Sentencing Transcripts, and judgment and commitment order;
11. Appellant Brief (if one was filed);
12. Appellee Brief (if any was filed);
13. Judgment of Court of Appeals.

<u>DOCUMENTS NEEDED TO CONTEST A JURY TRIAL:</u>

1. Investigative reports, Police Reports, ATF Reports, DEA 5 to 5 Reports, FBI Reports;
2. Search Warrants, Arrest Warrants and Affidavits used to obtain said Warrants;
3. Indictment and Information;
4. Docket Entry Sheet;
5. Motion to Suppress and any and all other pre-trial motions:
6. Suppression and hearing motion transcripts;
7. Proposed jury instructions by defense counsel;
8. Trial transcripts, including but not limited to, jury selection, opening arguments, trial, motions hearing held during the course of the trial, closing arguments and sentencing;
9. Jury Instruction charge;
10. Verdict form requested and the verdict form actually used at trial;

11. Motion for New Trial, if one filed also judgment for acquittal or arrest of judgment;

12. Transcripts related to hearing on motions for new Trial, judgment of acquittal, or arrest of judgment;

13. PSI Reports, along with any objections to PSI Reports;

14. Sentencing Transcripts and judgment of commitment order;

15. Notice of Appeal;

16. Appellant and Appellee Brief;

17. The Court of Appeals Opinion/Order;

18. All post-conviction motions if any exists;

19. Any letters from the prisoner to his or her attorney; or back to prisoner from his or her attorney;

20. Affidavits from witnesses who were not called and what their testimony would have been at trial, if they had been called;

21. Affidavits from other attorneys contesting the representation of the complained of attorney;

22. Affidavits from any expert witnesses if any and what their testimony would have been; and

23. Any affidavits or evidence withheld by the prosecutor if any.

The above listed documents are needed in order to prepare your Federal Writs under 28 U.S.C. §§ 2254 or 2255. The burden of proof in all writ proceeding rest on the Petitioner not the Government. Therefore, it is very important that you have all documentation as listed if you expect to have any chance at success.

GOOD LUCK.

CHAPTER: 1

SUPREME COURT CASES ON PROSECUTORIAL MISCONDUCT

LEADING CASES:

Massiah-V-United States, 377 U.S. 201, 204 (1964);
(A defendant's Sixth Amendment right is violated when the government uses other inmates to elicit incriminating statements from the defendant).

United States-V-Young,470 U.S. 1, 18-19 (1985);
(It is a due process violation for the prosecutor to vouch for the credibility of any witness).

Griffen-V-Cali., 380 U.S. 609, 615 (1965);
(failure of accused to testify in trial shall not be used against him before the jury by the prosecutor).

Blackledge-V-Perry, 417 U.S. 21, 28-29 (1974);
(improper for prosecutor to bring more serious charge 1n response to defendant invoking his statutory right to appeal).

Mooney-V-Holohan, 294 U.S. 103, 55 S.CT. 340 (1945);
(the Supreme Court first established the general proposition that a prosecutor's knowing and intended use of perjured testimony violated due process).

Giglio-V-United States, 405 U.S. 150, 153-154 (1972);
(clarifying that the rule stated in Brady applies to evidence undermining witness credibility).

United States-V-Agurs, 427 U.S. 97, 113 (1976);
("[i]f the verdict is already of questionable validity, additional evidence of relatively minor importance might be sufficient to create a reasonable doubt).

Kyles-V-Whitley, 514 U.S. 419, 441 (1995);
(requiring a "cumulating evaluation" of the materiality of wrongfully withheld evidence).

Porter-V-McCollum, 558 U.S. 30, 43 (2009);
(it was not reasonable to discount entirely the effect that [a defendant's expert's] testimony might have had on jury, just because the state's expert provided contrary testimony).

Brady-V-Maryland, 373 U.S. 83 (1963);
(due process violated by withholding exculpatory evidence at punishment phase of trial).

Youngblood-V-West Virginia, 547 U.S. 867, 869-70 (2006);
(Brady suppression occurs when the government fails to turn over evidence known only to the police investigators and not the prosecutor).

Weary-v-Cain, 136 S.CT. 1002 (2016);
(due process violation when prosecutor withheld deal made with jailhouse

informant).

United States-V-Henry, 447 U.S. 264, 270-71, 100 S.CT. 218, 65 L.ED.2d 115 (1980);

(holding: that the use of testimony by a fellow inmate, who is a paid informant acting under the instructions of government agents violate the Sixth Amendment right to counsel).

Main-V-Moulton, 474 U.S. 159, 106 S.CT. 477, 88 L.ED.2d 481 (1985);

(the court held that the recorded statements by Moulton should have been suppressed stating that the Sixth Amendment right to counsel having attached when he pleaded not guilty in State Court, the police knowingly circumvented Moulton's right to have counsel present at a confrontation between him and his co-defendant who was deemed to be an agent of the police).

CHAPTER: 2

IT IS IMPROPER FOR A PROSECUTOR TO USE ANOTHER INMATE AS AN AGENT OF THE STATE

CASES

United States-V-Lozada-Rivera, 177 F.3d 98, 106 (1st Cir. 1999);
(the government may not use a defendant's words against him at trial if those words "were deliberately elicited from him after he had indicated he wanted an attorney).

United States-V-Bender, 221 F.3d 265, 268 (2000);
(a person is "denied the basic protections of [the sixth amendment's]" guaranteed when there was used against him at his trial evidence of his own incriminating words, which federal agents had deliberately elicited from him after he had been indicted and in the absence of counsel).

United States-V-Feliz: 20 F.Supp.2d 97, 106 (D.ME. 1998);
(the sixth amendment right to counsel attaches when a defendant has been indicted).

United States-V-Melendez-Santiogo, 544 F.Supp.2d 76, 80 (D. Puerto 2007);
(the Supreme Court of the United States has held that a defendant's sixth amendment right to counsel is violated when the evidence used against him during trial consists "of his own incriminating words, which federal agents had deliberately elicited from him after he had been indicted and in the absence of his counsel").

Grievance Committee for Southern Dist. of New York-V-Simels, 48 F.3d 640, 647 (2nd Cir. 1995);
(in Massiah, 307 F.2d at 66 it was assumed without deciding that, if Dr 7-1049A)(1) applied to criminal investigations, it would not bar post-indictment contracts with represented defendants by investigatory agencies not acting as the prosecutor's alter ego).

United States-V-Miller, 116 F.3d 641, 665 (2nd Cir. 1997);
(it is well settled that the sixth amendment right to counsel is violated when a private individual, acting as a government agent, "deliberately elicit[s]" incriminating statements from an accused in the absence of his counsel)(citing Massiah-V-United States, 377 U.S. 201, 206, 84 S.CT. 1199, 1203, 12 L.ED.2d 245 (1964)).

United States-V-Rommy, 506 F.3d 108, 135 (2nd Cir. 2007);
(sixth amendment "covers only those statements obtained as a result of an intentional effort" on the part of the government officials to secure incriminating statements from the accused).

United States-V-Stein, 541 F.3d 130, 154 (2nd Cir. 2008);

([a]t the very least, the prosecutor and police have an affirmative obligation not to act in a manner that circumstances and thereby dilutes the production afforded by the right to counsel).

United States-V-Witten, Bollock, Rodriguez, Brown and Wilson, 610 F.3d 168, 193 (2nd Cir. 2010);

(the sixth amendment is violated when an informant becomes a government agent vis-a-vis a defendant when the informant IS "instructed by the police to get information about the particular defendant).

United States-V-Jacques, 684 F.3d 324, 330 (2nd Cir. 2012);

("[a]fter the right to counsel attaches and is invoked, any statements obtained from the accused during subsequent police-initiated custodial questioning regarding the charge at issue (citing McNeil V-Wisconsin, 501 U.S. 171, 179, 111 S.CT. 2204, 115 L.ED.2d 158 (1991)).

United States-V-Wilson, 493 F.Supp.2d 514, 515 (E.D.N.Y. 2007);

(the Massiah rule covers only those statements obtained as a result of an intentional effort on the part of the government, so information gotten before the inmates became agents/informants is not protected by the rule).

Smith-V-Fischer, 967 F.Supp.2d 418, 421 (S.D.N.Y. 2013);

(interrogations by the State constitutes a critical stage for the sixth amendment).

United States-V-Arnold, 106 F.3d 37, 42 (3rd Cir. 1997);

(the court held that Arnold's sixth amendment right to counsel, which attached to the witness intimidation charge on the morning of March 28th when he was indicted, carried over to the attempted murder of a witness charge. Consequently, the incriminating statements elicited from Arnold during the "sting" operation on the afternoon of March 28th were obtained in violation of Arnold's sixth amendment right to counsel, and the District Court erred by failing to suppress the tape recording).

Mattes-V-Superintendant, SCI Albion, 171 F.3d 877, 905 (3rd Cir. 1999);

(the sixth amendment right to counsel was violated, but held harm less do to overwhelming evidence).

Davis-V-Township of Paulboro, 421 F.Supp.2d 835, 847 (D.N.J. 2006);

(any potential violation of Davis, Sixth Amendment right must have occurred after criminal charges were formally initiated against him).

United States-V-Lentz, 524 F.3d 501, 520 (4th Cir. 2008);

(the mere presence of a jailhouse informant who had been instructed to overhear conversations and to engage a criminal defendant in some conversations [is] not necessarily unconstitutional).

United States-V-Mir., 525 F.3d 351, 355 (4th Cir. 2008);

(thus, "government investigations of new criminal activity for which an accused has not been indicted do not violate the Sixth Amendment right to counsel").

United States-V-Smith, 623 F.Supp.2d 693 (U.S. Dist. 2009);

(a defendant does not make out a violation of [his sixth amendment] right simply by showing that an informant, either through prior arrangement or voluntarily, reported his incriminating statements to the police. Rather, the defendant must demonstrate that the police and their informant took some action, beyond merely listening that was designed deliberately to elicit incriminating remarks. **Kuhlmann-V-Wilson**, 477, U.S. 436, 459, 106 S.CT. 2516, 91 L.ED.2d 364 (1986) (emphasis added).

Olive-V-New Jersey, 579 F.Supp.2d 643 (3 Dist. New Jersey 2008);

(sixth amendment right to counsel attaches at the initiation of formal charges).

Blackman-V-Johnson, 145 F.3d 205, 210 (5th Cir. 1998);

(when an agent does more than just listen, but also initiates discussion of the case which leads to incriminating statements, a sixth amendment violation occurs).

Henderson-V-Quarterman, 460 F.3d 654, 664 (5th Cir. 2006);

(the sixth amendment right to counsel under Massiah is offense can not be violated until sixth amendment specific, this right protection attaches).

United States-V-McAuliffs, 490 F.3d 526, 539 (6th Cir. 2007);

("once the sixth amendment right attaches, any governmental attempt to elicit information from the accused without the defendant's lawyer present, even through means that maybe permissible under the fifth amendment right to counsel prior to the point at which the sixth amendment right to counsel attaches (e.g. electronic monitoring of a suspects conversations with others)(affirmed for other reasons).

Brooks-V-Tennessee, 626 F.3d 878, 897 (6th Cir. 2010);

(the Supreme Court in Massiah-V-United States, 377 U.S. 201 (1964), held that a criminal defendant is denied the sixth amendment right to counsel where the prosecution "use[s] against him at his trial evidence of his own incriminating words, which federal agents... deliberately elicited from him after he had been indicted and in the absence of his counsel." Id. at 206. This rule applies where the government recruits an undercover jailhouse informant, or other wise "intentionally create[s] a situation likely to induce [a defendant] to make incriminating statements without the assistance of counsel." United States-V-Henry, 447 U.S. 264, 274 (1980)).

Alexander-V-Smith, 343 F.Supp.2d 677, 587 (E.D. Mich. 2004);

("[t]he sixth amendment is violated when the State obtains incriminating statements by knowingly circumventing the accused's right to have counsel present in a confrontation between the accused and a State agent." Main-V-Moulton, 474 U.S. 159, 176 (1985); see also Massiah-V-United States, 377 U.S. 201, 206 (1964) (Holding: that the basic protections of the sixth amendment were violated when incriminating statements deliberately elicited from the petitioner after he had been indicted but in the absence of counsel, were used against him at trial).

United States-V-Kallstrom, 446 F.Supp.2d 772, 776 (E.D. Mich. 2006);

(one's spelling acumen is different than the characteristics of one's handwriting. To convey the former, communication must take place, which, in a custodial setting and after an arraignment has taken place, cannot be canceled absent a valid waiver. See Smith V-Arizona, 451 U.S. 477, 484-85 (1981)); Massiah-V-United States, 377 U.S. 201, 204 (1964)).

United States-V-Li., 55 F.3d 325, 328 (7th Cir. 1995);

(Massiah-V-United States., establishes that the sixth amendment prohibits the government from deliberately eliciting incriminating statements from a defendant, in the absence of counsel, after the defendant has been indicted. 377 U.S. 201, (1964). To find a sixth amendment violation, the statements in question must have been (1) deliberately elicited (2) by a government agent).

United States-V-Carrillo, 20 F.Supp.2d 854, 861 (N.D. Ill. 1999);

(specifically, the exclusionary rule operates to suppress evidence where the government has violated an individual's constitutional rights under the Fourth, Fifth or Sixth Amendments. See Miranda V-Arizona, 384 U.S. 436 (1966) (Fifth Amendment). Massiah-V-Unitecl States, 377 U.S. 201 (1964)(sixth amendment); Mapp-V-Ohio, 367 U.S. 643 (196l)(Fourth Amendment).

United States-V-Barrogan-Rangel, 198 F.Supp.2d 973, 977 (N.D. Ill. 2002);

(Massiah's prohibition does not apply to statements, such as solicitation of a bribe (or in this case, witness tampering), that are not statements of past conduct but are themselves criminal acts).

Beck-V-Bowersox, 363 F.3d 1095, 1105 (8th Cir. 2004);

(criminal defendant's are guaranteed the right to counsel at all critical stages of criminal proceedings, the right attaches to "interrogation activities conducted at or after the initiation of adversary criminal proceeding-whether by way of formal charge, preliminary hearing, indicted or information or arraignment.") (Citing Gilmore-V-Armontout, 861 F.2d 1061, 1070 (8th Cir. 1988) (quoting Kirby-V-Illinoise, 406 U.S. 682, 689, 92 S.CT. 1877, 32 L.ED.2d 411 (1972))).

United States-V-Chahia, 544 F.3d 890, 899 (8th Cir. 2008);

(in Massiah-V-U.S., 377 U.S. 201, (1964), the Supreme Court deter mined that the sixth amendment rights of a defendant were violated "when there was used against him at trial evidence of his own incriminating words which federal agents has deliberately elicited from him after he had been indicted and in the absence of his counsel."). id at 206.

Dowell-V-Lincoln County, 927 F.Supp.2d 741, 753 (E. Dist. Miss. 2013); (Massiah quoted various authorities indicating that the violation occurred at the moment of the post-indictment interrogation... but the opinion later supported that the violation occurred only when the improperly obtained evidence was used against [the defendant] at his trial).

United States-V-Danielson. 325 F.3d 1054, 1067 (9th Cir-. 2003);

(any statements so gathered must be excluded from the government's case-in-chief, although "they are admissible to impeach conflicting testimony by the defendant's," provided the statements were voluntary).

Randolph-V-People of the State of Cal., 380 F.3d 1133, 1138 (9th Cir. 2004);

(we hold that if the government places a cooperating informant in a jail cell with a defendant whose right to counsel has attached, and if the informant then makes a successful effort to stimulate a conversation with the defendant about a crime charged, the State thereby violates the defendant's sixth amendment rights under Massiah).

-10-

Shillinger-V-Haworth, 70 F.3d 1132, 1142 (10th Cir. 1995);

("cases involving sixth amendment deprivation are subject to the general rule that remedies should be tailored to the injury suffered from the constitutional violation and should not unnecessarily infringe on competing interests").

United States-V-Johnson, 4 F.3d 904, 910 (10th Cir. 1993);

("[i]n order' to find a violation of a defendant's sixth amendment right to counsel, a court must find that defendant's statement (1) were made to a government agent, and (2) were deliberately elicited.").

Gore-V-Secretary for Dept. of Corrections, 492 F.3d 1273, 1303 (11th cir. 2007);

(Fellers-V-United States, 540 U.S. 519, 523, 124 S.CT. 1019, 1022 (2004) ("[a]n accused is denied the basic protections of the sixth Amendment when there [is] used against him at his trial evidence of his own incriminating words, which [law enforcement] agents... deliberately elicited from him after he had been indicted and in the absence of his counsel." (quoting Massiah, 377 U.S. at 206, 84 S.CT. at 1203)).

Hannon-V-Secretary, Department of Corrections, 622 F.2d 1169, 1217 (U.S. Dist. Ct. Mid. Dist. Florida, Tampa Div. 2007);

(Citing U.S.-V-Massiah, 377 U.S. 201, 84 S.CT. 1199 (1964)(using jailhouse informant to elicit incriminating information outside of counsel violates the Sixth Amendment).

Beatriz Marrero-V-United States, 676 F.Supp.2d 1334, 1339 fn.4 (U.S. Dist. Court Southern Dist. Florida 2009);

(defense counsel may file a motion to suppress post arrest statements obtained in violation of the Massiah doctrine).

United States-V-Bourdet. 477 F.3d 164, 183 (D.C. Cir. 2007);

("[w]hen the government opposes a motion to suppress a confession, it need prove waiver only by a preponderance of the evidence").

CHAPTER: 3

IT IS IMPROPER FOR A PROSECUTOR TO EXPRESS PERSONAL OPINIONS ABOUT THE DEFENDANT'S GUILT OR CREDIBILITY

CASES:

United States-V-Smith, 982 F.2d 681, 684 (1ˢᵗ Cir. 19-93);
(prosecutor's statement that defendant was guilty improper because implied personal belief rather than governments position).

United Statea-V-Auch, 137 F.3d 125, 131 (1ˢᵗ Cir. 1999);
(prosecutor's statement, "[t]he only way I can even imagine ever acquitting this man…" improper because it conveyed personal opinion).

United States-V-Andujar-Basco, 488 F.3d 549, 561 (1st Cir. 2007);
(prosecutor's personal opinion that defendant is guilty was improper but no harm shown).

United States-V-Gonzales-Vargas, 550 F.2d 631, 632-3 (1st Cir. 1977);
(vacating a conviction where the prosecutor stated his personal belief in summation about the defendant's guilt).

United States-V-Williams, 690 F.3d 70, 76 (2nd Cir. 2012);
(prosecutor's statements vouching for the credibility of witnesses generally improper because they imply the existence of evidence not placed before the jury, and because prosecutorial vouching carries with it imprimatur of the government and may induce the jury to trust the government's judgment rather than its own view of the evidence).

United States-V-Certified Unvtl., Serv. Inc., 753 F.3d 72, 94-95 (2nd Cir. 2014);
(prosecutor's statement, "I assure you, he has more to do than he knows what to do with," Improper because it implied personal belief).

United States-V-Maldonado, 882   F.2d 463, 479 (U.S. Dist. Court Southern Dist. NY. 2011);
(in evaluating a claim of improper argument, a court must consider the objectionable remarks within the context of the entire trial, granting relief only if the remarks, viewed against the entire argument only deprived the defendant of a fair trial).

Arena-V-Kaplan, 952 F.Supp.2d 468, 479 (U.S. Dist. Court Eastern Dist. NY 2013);
(improper remarks by a prosecutor during, the course of a criminal trial can rise to the level of an unconstitutional deprivation of the right to a fair trial. To establish a constitutional violation, the improper remarks must have so infected the trial with unfairness as to make the resulting conviction a denial of due process).

United States-V-Zehrbech. 47 F.3d 1252, 1269 (3rd Cir. 1995);

(prosecutor's statement that jury should disbelieve defense because they were guilty of same fraud as to defendant's improper).

United States-V-Jimenez, 513 F.3d 62, 84 (3rd Cir. 2003);

(the district court found the comments by the prosecutor to be an attack on the defendant and his counsel. However, this was cured by the court instructing the prosecutor to apologize to counsel before the jury).

United States-V-Georgiou, 742 F.Supp.2d 613, 636 (U.S. Dist. Ct. E. Dist. Penn. 2010);

(it is well settled that a prosecutor's comments constitute reversible error only if they are so erroneous as to undermine the fundamental fairness of the trial and contribute to a miscarriage of justice. Further, [i]nappropriate prosecutorial comments, standing alone, would not justify a reviewing court to reverse a criminal conviction obtained in an otherwise fair proceeding).

Boyd-V-French, 147 F.3d 319, 328-29 (4th Cir. 1998);

(prosecutor's statements during closing argument regarding personal opinion of defendant's credibility improper).

United States-V-Woods, 710 F.3d 195, 202-03 (4th Cir. 2013);

(prosecutor's statement that defendant and lied under oath improper because inflammatory).

United States-V-Duffaut, 314 F.3d 203, 210-11 (5th Circ. 2002);

(prosecutor's statement that he did not believe that having drugs was "okay" improper though remedied by contemporaneous curative instruction).

United States-V-Garcia, 522 F.3d 597, 601 (5th Cir. 2008);

(court held it was improper comment for the prosecutor to vouch for the credibility of witnesses).

Hodge-V-Burley, 426 F. 3d 368, 377 (6th Cir. 2005);

(prosecutor's statement that defendant was lying especially when contracted with comment that government witness absolutely believable, improper).

Girts-V-Yanai, 501 F.3d 743, 759 (6th Cir. 2007);

(prosecutor's comment improper where he commented on the defendants failure to testify)

Cristini-V-McKee, 526 F.3d 888, 901-02 (6th Cir. 2008);

(improper for prosecutor to call defense witnesses liars, but held harmless).

United States-V-Warshak, 631 F.3d 266, 303 (6th Cir. 2010);

(prosecutor's statement that defendants were weak and sought money at expense of public improper because it implied personal belief of guilt).

United States-V-Nunez, 532 F.3d 645, 653 (7th Cir. 2008);

(prosecutor's statement that defendant's testimony was "patently false" and "unresponsive to the question" was improper personal opinion).

United States-V-Milbourn, 600 F.3d 908, 812 (7th Cir. 2010);

(to prevail on a claim that the prosecutor engages in misconduct during closing arguments, petitioner must establish ("not only that the remarks denied him a fair trial, but also that the outcome of the proceedings would have been different absent the remarks")).

United States-V-Tucker, 714 F.3d 1006, 1016 (7th Cir. 2013);

(the appellate court focuses on the ("probable effect the prosecutor's [remarks] would have on the jury's ability to judge the evidence fairly")).

Braun-V-Powell, 77 F.Supp.2d 973, 1000 (E.D. Wis. 1999);

(in cases where prosecutorial misconduct is alleged, the ('touchstone of due process… is the fairness of the trial with unfairness as to make the resulting conviction a denial of due process')).

Keller-V-McCann, 553 F.Supp.2d 1002 (E.D. x11. 2008);

(a prosecutor's comments must ("so infect the trial with unfairness as to make the resulting conviction a denial of due process")).

United States-V-Holmes, 413 F.3d 770, 774-75 (8th Cir. 2005);

(court found it improper for prosecutor to attack defense counsel's credibility).

United States-V-Green, 580 F.3d 353, 859 (6th Cir. 2009);

(prosecutor's remarks that he had other witnesses he could have called was improper, but curative instruction by judge cured error).

United State-V-Miller, 621 F.3d 723, 730-32 (8th Circ. 2010);

(the court concluded that a prosecutor's argument than an acquittal would have required the jury to find that a police officer was ["fudging"] and willing to jeopardize his future career, was improper).

United States-V-Thomas, 664 F.3d 217, 224 (8th Cir. 2011);

(prosecutor's statement, "if this isn't a first degree murder case, ladies and gentleman, I don't know what is," improper).

United States-V-Darden, 588 F.3d 382, 392-93 (8th Cir. 2012);

(J. Mallow in his dissent found prosecutor's remarks that for jury to acquit the defendant means the officer is lying improper).

United States-V-Garcia-Buizar, 160 F.3d 511, 520 (9th Cir. 1998);

(prosecutor's statement describing defendant as a "liar" improper because personal opinion regarding defendant's credibility).

United States-V-Kojayan, 8 F.36 1315, 1318-19 (9th Circ. 1993);

(the court reversed the conviction based on a prosecutor's misstatement that the government was powerless to compel a witness to testify when, in fact, the witness had entered into a plea agreement with the government and had promised to testify at trial).

United States-V-Weatherspoon, 410 F.3d 1142, 1147-1151 (9th Cir. 2005);

(it was improper for the prosecutor to vouch for the credibility of witnesses and expressing his personal opinion concerning the guilt of the accused).

United States-V-Wright, 625 F.3d 583, 611 (9th Cir. 2010);

(prosecutor's numerous references to his own impression, including "I think what the defendant said… was so completely illogical it was absolutely ridiculous," were improper personal opinions).

Cargle-V-Mullins, 317 F.3d 1196, 1218 (10th Cir.   2003);

(prosecutor's statement that state does not prosecute innocent people improper because "[i]t is always improper for a prosecutor to suggest that a defendant is guilty merely because he is being prosecuted" (quoting United States-V-Boss, 593 F.2d 749, 754 (6th Cir. 1979))).

United States-V-Lopez-Medina, 596 F.3d 710, 740 (10th Cir. 2010);

(prosecutor's statement connecting defendant's weight gain with cessation of methamphetamine use improper personal opinion because no testimony about connection at trial).

United States-V-Mueller, 74 F.3d 1152, 1157 (11th Cir. 1996);

(prosecutor's statement that defendant lied in various forms improper).

United States-V-Frank, 599 F.3d 1221, 1228 (11th Cir. 2010);

(a defendant's substantial rights are prejudicially effected when a reasonable probability arises that but for the comment [of the prosecutor] the outcome [of the trial] would have been different).

United States-V-Madden, 733 F.3a 1314, 1320 (11th Cir. 2013);

(a prosecutor's argument [remarks] must seriously effect the fairness, integrity or public reputation of judicial proceedings).

McNair-V-Campbell, 607 F.Supp.2d 1277, 1327 (M.D. Ala. 2004);

(the Supreme Court has noted that it can be improper for a prosecutor to exert presume on a jury by exhorting it to "do its job").

Ford-V-Schield, 488 F.Supp.2d 1258, 1327 (N.D. GA. 2007);

(in United States-V-Young, 470 U.S. 1, 18 (1985), the Supreme Court found that it may be error for a prosecutor to exert presume on the jury by urging the jury to "do its job").

Ogle-V-Johnson, 696 F.Supp.2d 1345, 1368 (S.D. Ga. 2009);

(the United States Supreme Court has established that a prosecutor [must refrain from interjecting personal beliefs into the presentation of his case]).

United States-V-Brown, 508 F.3d 1066, 1075 (D.C. Cir. 2007);

(impermissible vouching is particularly dangerous when it is done by prosecutors: Juries are aware that prosecutors have ("as much [a] duty to refrain from improper methods calculated to produce a wrongful conviction as [they have] to use every legitimate means to bring about from giving his personal opinion").

CHAPTER: 4

IT IS IMPROPER FOR THE PROSECUTOR TO MAKE REMARKS ABOUT THE DEFENDANT

STANDARD OF REVIEW:

Donnelly-V-Christofor, 416 U.S. 537, 643, 94 S.CT. 1868, 40 L.ED.2d 431 (1974)

(the Supreme Court has recognized that prosecutorial misconduct may "so infect the trial with unfairness as to make the resulting conviction a denial of due process").

Darden-V-Wainwright, 477 U.S. 168, 180-81, 106 S.CT. 2464, 91 L.ED.2d 144 (1986);

(improper remarks by a prosecutor during the course of a criminal trial can rise to the level of an unconstitutional deprivation of the right to a fair trial).

CASES:

United States-V-Martinez-Medina, 279 F.3d 105, 119 (1st Cir. 2002);

(prosecutor's reference's to defendant's as "hunting each other like animals" and "killing one another with no mercy" improper).

Olszevski-V-Spencer, 465 F.3d 47 (1st Cir. 2006);

("the prosecutor's remarks that the defendant was guilty, error, but cured by curative instruction").

United States-V-Ayala-Garcia, 574 F.3d 5, 17 (1st Cir. 2009);

(it was improper for the prosecutor to tell jury that 31 lives were saved invoking the 31 bullets that way, while also urging jurors to consider their size could have served no purpose other than to inflame the jury's passion by depicting the defendants as dangerous men who needed to be put away for a long time).

United States-V-Kinsella, 622 F.3d 75, 85-86 (1st Cir. 2010);

(prosecutor's reference to drug sales unsupported by evidence improper).

United States-V-Rodriquez, 675 F.3d 51, 61-62 (1st Cir. 2012);

(it was improper for the prosecutor to state "the defendant acted like a guilty man." No prejudice shown).

Miranda-V-Bennett, 322 F.3d 171, 150-81 (2nd Cir. 2003);

(it was improper for the prosecutor to present to the jury the defendant's wallet, and arguing that it was stolen from robbery victim. This implied the defendant was guilty).

United States-V-Newton, 369 F.3d 144, 154-56 (2nd Cir. 2004);

(prosecutor's closing statement asking if jury would trust defendant with jury improper).

United States-V-Yakobowiez, 427 F.3d 141, 154-56 (2nd Cir. 2005);

(improper for the prosecutor to make comment's after each witnesses testimony was structural error requiring reversal).

United States-V-Burden, 600 F.3d 204, 221-22 (2nd Cir. 2010);
(prosecutor's comparison between Al-Qaeda and defendants narcotics organization improper).

United States-V-Irizany, 341 F.3d 273, 308 (3rd Cir. 2003);
(prosecutor's attempt during questioning to associate defendant with rebuttal emphasized crime boss improper).

United States-V-Moore, 375 F.3d 259, 264-65 (3rd Cir. 2004);
(prosecutor's statement that defendant was a 'terrorist' improper).

Fahy-V-Horn, 516 F.3d 169, 201-02 (3rd Cir. 2008);
(it was improper for the prosecutor to suggest that the defendant is a representative of Lucifer or Satan, but deemed harmless because in response to counsel's summation).

United States-V-Weatherless, 734 F.2d 179, 181 (4th Cir. 196);
(prosecutor's remarks referring to defendant as a "rapist," "liar," "loser," "sick man," and as someone who "couldn't even ejaculate" clearly improper).

Humphries-V-Ozmint, 366 F.3d 266, 237 (4th Cir. 2004);
(prosecutor's closing argument at capital sentencing hearing, which compared the respective worth of the life of murder victim to that of petitioner, rendered trail fundamentally unfair in violation of due process).

United States-V-Humprey, 506 F.3d 214, 227 (4th Cir. 2010);
(it was improper for prosecutor to state to the jury in closing that defendant funded terrorism, but no prejudice shown).

Hall-V-United States, 419 F.2d 582, 537-88 (5th Cir. 1969);
(prosecutor's statement that defendant was a "hoodlum" improper).

Bates-V-Bell, 402 F.3d 635, 641-42 (6th Cir. 2005);
(it was improper during summation for the Coffee County prosecutor to continually tell the jury that they would "become an accomplice to his crime by permitting this man to live," and argued that the jury would be responsible for the future deaths of other if they opted to sentence Bates to life imprisonment rather than death).

Hodge-V-Hurley, 426 F.3d 386, 389 (6th Cir. 2005);
(prosecutor's statement improper because related to crime charged and inappropriately emphasized defendant's character).

United States-V-Wettstain, 618 F.3d 577,589 (6th Cir. 2010);
(prosecutor's labeling of defendant as "monsters" improper).

United States Ex rel. Clark-V-Fike, 528 F.2d 750, 759 (7th Cir. 1976);
(prosecutor's statement defendant engaged in criminal activity "every other night" improper).

United States-V-Hale, 448 F.3d 971, 986-88 (7th Cir. 2006);
(prosecutor's statement that defendant had member of his organization kill two (2) people improper).

United States-V-Stinefoot, 724 F.3d 925, 930 (7th Cir. 2013);
(to succeed under the plan error standard, Stinefoot first must show that prosecutor's comments "were obviously or clearly improper" if the remarks were blatantly improper Stinefoot must also demonstrate that the statement prejudiced him).

Geiger-V-Cain, 540 F.3d 303, 308 (5th Cir. 2008);
(comments by the prosecutor during voir dire were improper, but no prejudice shown).

Rish-V-Thompson, 959 F.Supp.2d 1096, 1115 (C.D. 2013);
(the Supreme Court has stated that "the relevant question is whether the prosecutor's comments so infected the trial with unfairness as to make the resulting conviction a denial of due process").

United States-V-Carter, 410 F.3d 1017, 1026 (8th Cir. 2005);
(prosecutor's comments calling defendant "can man" and "deviate [sic]" improper, but because evidence was substantial, comments did not justify reversal).

United States-V-Montgomery, 635 F.3d 1074, 1097-98 (8th Cir. 2011);
(prosecutor's criticism of defendant's decision to have her children testify improper).

United States-V-Dunn, 723 F.3d 919, 933 (8th Cir. 2013);
(when considering a new trial motion based on ambiguous remarks in closing argument, "a court should not lightly infer that a prosecutor intends on ambiguous remarks have its most damaging meaning or that a jury, sitting through lengthy exertion will draw that meaning from plethora of less damaging interpretations").

Allen-V-Woodford, 395 F.3d 979, 1016 (9th Cir. 2005);
(prosecutor's comparison to "Adolf Hitler" improper).

United States-V-Weatherspoon, 410 F.3d 1142, 1152-53 (9th Cir. 2005);
(it was improper for the prosecutor to tell jury to convict to alleviate social problems regarding the defendant).

Hein-Y-Sullivan, 601 F.3d 897, 913 (9th Cir. 2010);
(prosecutor's comparison of defendants to "a pack of wolves" and calling one defendant "a little punk" improper).

Malicoat-V-Mullin, 426 F.3d 1241, 1256 (10th Cir. 2005);
(prosecutor's comment calling defendant "evil" and "a monster" improper).

Hamilton-V-Mullin, 436 F.3d 1181, 1188 (10th Cir. 2006);

(prosecutor's comment "the cloak of innocence is stripped away" improper, but harmless do to overwhelming evidence).

United States-V-Blekey, 14 F.3d 1557, 1559-60 (11th Cir. 1994);

(prosecutor's statement that defendant was "professional criminal," improper when contrary facts existed).

Davis-V-Zant, 36 F.3d 1538, 1547 (11th Cir. 1994);

(improper statement of evidence telling the jury that the defense "thought up" during trial that Underwood and not Davis had killed and confessed months earlier to the murders).

Cargill-V-Turpin, 120 F.3d 1366, 1381 (11th Cir. 1997);

(improper statement to jury by prosecutor: "Is that all the jury thought of my mama and daddy because that man is sitting off some where eating Christmas Turkey dinner?").

United States-V-Wilson, 149 F.3d 1298, 1300-01 (11th Cir. 1998);

(prosecutor's characterization of defendant as a "major drug dealer" improper where only indicted for a single sale of small amount of cocaine).

CHAPTER: 5

IT IS IMPROPER FOR THE PROSECUTOR TO MAKE REMARKS ABOUT DEFENSE COUNSEL

CASES:

United States-V-Boldt, 929 F.2d 35, 40 (1st Cir. 1991);
(prosecutor's remarks that it's a "favor-able defense tactic to try to get [the jury] to focus on unnecessary facts or to get [the jury] emotionally wrapped up with the defendant" was improper because it casts suspicion on the general role of defense counsel rather than a theory of the case).

United States-V-Manning, 23 F.3d 570, 573 n.l (1st Cir. 1994);
(disproving of prosecutor's remark that defense counsel were like "Shakespeare's players, full of sound and fury signifying nothing").

United States-V-Procopio, 88 F.3d 21, 32 (1st Cir. 1996);
(the prosecutor told the jury that defense arguments where "illusions a smoke screen aimed at creating that, an illusion to deflect you from a single thread of truth that... unifies all the evidence in this case." improper).

United States-V-Friedman, 909 F.2d 705, 708 (2nd Cir. 1990);
(prosecutor's statement that defense counsel would "make any argument he can to get the guy off" and that "while some people prosecute drug dealers there are others who... "try to get them off, perhaps even for high fees" improper).

United States-V-Olliverre, 378 F.3d 412, 417-21 (4th Cir. 2004);
(prosecutor's statement it "is just incredible that [defense counsel] can say that [government has no proof] with a straight face, incredible" improper).

United States-V-Vaccaro, 115 F.3d 1211, 1218 (5th Cir. 1997);
(prosecutor's statement that defense lawyers "muddle the issues" improper).

Bates-V-Bell, 402 F.3d 635, 647 (6th Cir. 2005);
(prosecutor's response "[i]t's just getting too close for you" and subsequent response to defense counsel's objections improper because criticized defense counsel for protecting client and were aimed at prejudicing defendant's right to object).

United States-V-Davis, 514 F.3d 598, 616 (6th Cir. 2008):
(Cook stated that it was "offensive" for defense counsel to argue that public servants who "risk their lives everyday" would fabricate evidence or lie)(error shown but not egregious).

Pierson-V-O'Leary, 959 F.2d 1385, 1388 (7th Cir. 1992);
(prosecutor's remark claiming that defense counsel was "keeping the whole truth" from the jury improper).

United States-V-Rodriquez, 581 F.3d 775, 802 (8th Cir. 2009);
(prosecutor's statement that defense counsel was trying to "sell" the case improper).

United States-V-Rodriquez, 159 F.3d 439, 452 (9th Cir. 1998);
(prosecutor's statement that defense counsel had "tried to deceive [jury] from the start" improper).

Hein-V-Sullivan, 601 F.3d 897, 913 (9th Cir. 2010);
(prosecutor's remarks claiming that defense counsel was dishonest" and guilty of some "very dirty things" improper because a personal attack against defense counsel's character).

Johnson-Y-Gibson, 169 F.3d 1239, 1250 (10th Cir. 1999);
(prosecutor's flat statements about defense counsel improper).

United States-V-Frazier, 944 F.2d 820, 827 (11th Cir. 1991);
(prosecutor's statement1 "the defense... was garbage" improperly maligned defendant's counsel).

CHAPTER: 6

IT IS IMPROPER FOR A PROSECUTOR TO MAKE REMARKS ABOUT A DEFENSE WITNESSES

CASES:

United States-V-Modica, 663 F.2d 1173, 1179-80 (2nd Cir. 1981);
(prosecutor's statement regarding defense witnesses as "scared" improper).
United States-V-Zehrbach, 47 F.3d 1252, 1264 (3rd Cir. 1995);
(prosecutor's statement that two (2] witnesses guilty of same crime as defendant improper).
United States-V-Nitchell, 1 F.3d 235, 240 (4th Cir. 1993);
(prosecutor's argument that defendant's brother's testimony should be disbelieved because brother's own jury had disbelieved him improper).
United States-V-Thomas, 246 F.3d 438, 439 (5th Cir. 2001);
(prosecutor's declaration to jury that defense witness not telling truth improper).
Hodge-V-Hurley, 426 F.3d 368, 382-83 (6th Cir. 2005);
(prosecutor's statement suggesting defense witness acting wrongfully or unethically or was perjuring himself improper).
United States-V-Rutledge, 40 F.3d 879, 887 (7th Cir. 1994);
(prosecutor's remark that "defense should have been embarrassed to hear" defense witnesses testimony improper). Overruled on other grounds by Rutledge-V-United States, 517 U.S. 292 (1996).
Baker-V-United States, 115 F.2d 533, 543 (8th Cir. 1940);
(prosecutor's remark that defense witness was the "most desperate sort of man" and had a fraud order issued against him improper).
United States-V-Crutchfield, 26 F.3d 1098, 1101-02 (11th Cir. 1994);
(prosecutor's irrelevant questions insinuating defense witness involved in major drug operation and other misconduct improper).
United States-V-Young, 463 F.2d 934, 938 (D.C. Cir. 1972);
(prosecutor's remark concerning defendant's alibi witness's failure to contact police improper).

CHAPTER: 7

IT IS IMPROPER FOR A PROSECUTOR TO ASK A DEFENSE WITNESS TO COMMENT ON THE CREDIBILITY OF ANOTHER WITNESS

CASES:

United States-V-Robinson, 473 F.3d 387, 395 (1st Cir. 2007);
(prosecutor's cross-examination of defendant asking him whether two [2] law enforcement witnesses lied improper).

United States-V-Truman, 688 F.3d 129, 143 (2nd Cir. 2012);
(prosecutor's cross-examination of defendant asking him whether government witnesses were "mistaken or lying" improper).

United States-V-Nunez, 532 F.3d 645, 652 (7th Cir. 2008);
(prosecutor's cross-examination of defendant asking whether DEA AGENT WAS LYING IMPROPER).

United States-V-Moreland, 622 F.3d 1147, 1158-59 (9th Cir. 2010);
(prosecutor's cross-examination of defendant asking whether 2 government lied during their testimony improper).

United States-V-Schitz, 634 F.3d 1247, 1267-68 (11th Cir. 2011);
(prosecutor's cross-examination of defendant requiring him to say whether other witnesses lied improper).

United States-V-Boyd, 54 F.3d 868, 871 (D.C. Cir. 1995);
(prosecutor's remark as defendant on stand if other witnesses were lying improper).

CHAPTER: 8

IT IS IMPROPER FOR A PROSECUTOR TO EXPRESS PERSONAL OPINIONS REQUIRING EXPERT KNOWLEDGE

CASES:

United States-V-Lee, 612 F.3d 170, 195 (3rd Cir. 2010);
(prosecutor's comment about his own personal experience with dogs improper).

United States-V-McDonald, 905 F.2d 871, 875-76 (5th Cir. 1990);
(prosecutor's comment referring to defendant's custody battle improper because acting as expert witness on divorce and custody law).

Gall-V-Parker, 231 F.3d 265, 312 (6th Cir. 2000);
(prosecutor's suggestion jury heed his expertise as government prosecutor and dismiss defendant's insanity defense improper).

United States-V-Galloway, 316 F.3d 624, 632-33 (6th Cir. 2003);
(prosecutor's comment about his personal experience trying other cases involving drug mules improper).

United States-Y-Brown, 785 F.2d 587, 591 (7th Cir. 1986);
(prosecutor's criticism of Rorschach inkblot test relied on by defendant's expert witness improper).

United States-V-Mullins, 446 F.3d 750, 761 (8th Cir. 2006);
(prosecutor's statement that he test fired gun in evidence improper because acting as expert).

United States-V-Wright, 625 F.3d 583, 610-11 (9th Cir. 2010);
(prosecutor's comment about similar cases he tried improper because reflected prosecutor's impression of the evidence and induced prosecutor's personal experience).

Vance-V-Zant, 696 F.2d 940, 951 (11th Cir. 1983);
(prosecutor's remark citing to his prosecutor and explaining to jury experience as FBI agent and why people generally confess improper).

King-V-United States, 372 F.2d 383, 394 (D.C. Cir. 1966);
(prosecutor's remark that organic impairment of brain may not be based on psychological tests if it is not shown by physical examination improper expression of expert knowledge).

CHAPTER: 9

IT IS IMPROPER FOR A PROSECUTOR TO COMMENT ON A DEFENDANT'S FAILURE TO TESTIFY

CASES:

United States-V-Cormier, 469 F.2d 63, 73-74 (1st Cir. 2006);
(prosecutor's comments regarding defendant's "own words and actions" and "credibility" improper comment on the defendant's decision not to testify).

Gomes-V-Brady, 584 F.3d 532, 538 (1st Cir. 2009);
(prosecutor's comment that only defendant's attorney had taken the stand to argue that defendant and not committed the crime improper because "take the stand is a direct allusion to act of testifying).

United States-V-Martinez, 786 F.3d 121, 128 (1st Cir. 2015);
(it is well settled to warrant citation of authority that a prosecutor in closing argument may try to convince the jury of the force (or lack of force) of the testimony of particular witness. There is sometimes a fine line, however, between a permissible critique of witness's testimony and an impermissible comment on the defendant's silence. For that reason, we have warned that prosecutor's should tread with caution in this area)(United States-V-Sepulveda, 15 F.3d 1151, 1186 (1st Cir. 1993)).

Fox-V-Mann, 71 F.3d 66, 72 (2nd Cir. 1995);
(prosecutor's comment, "if the defendant wants to speak, he can take the stand," improper because it invited jury to draw negative inference from defendant's failure to testify).

United States-V-Sprengel, 103 F.2d 875, 883 (3rd Cir. 1989);
(prosecutor's comment that defendant failed to answer questionnaires sent to them improper because analogous to a comment upon their failure to testify).

Lesko-V-Lehman, 925 F.2d 1527, 1544 (3rd Cir. 1991);
(prosecutor's request that jury consider defendant's "arrogance" in failing to apologize for homicide improper).

Gangora-V-Thaler, 710 F.3d 207, 275 (5th Cir. 2013);
(prosecutor's comment "who should we go ahead and talk to? Who should we go ahead and present to you?" While pointing to defendant was improper).

DePew-V-Anderson, 311 F.3d 742, 749 (6th Cir. 2002);
(prosecutor's statement that defendant did not testify to avoid being asked about prior convictions improper).

Girts-V-Yanai, 501 F.3d 743, 758-61 (6th Cir. 2007);
(prosecutor's statement that defendant was the only person who could explain wife's death improper because prejudicial, repeated, and deliberate).

Moore-V-Mitchell, 708 F.3d 760, 800 (6th Cir. 2013);
(prosecutor's rhetorical question about why defendant did not explain his travel

decisions improper because drawing jury's attention to defendant's failure to testify).

Ben-Yisrayl-V-Davis, 431 F.3d 1043, 1059-51 (7th Cir. 2005);
(prosecutor's statement focusing on defendant's confession, retraction, and subsequent failure to testify improper because encouraged jury to infer guilt from defendant's silence).

United States-V-Phillips, 745 F.3d 829, 834 (7th Cir. 2014);
(the government violated a defendant's right against self-incrimination if "it manifestly intended to refer to her silence" when arguing to the jury) (quotation marks, citation, and brackets, omitted).

United States-V-Triplett, 795 F.3d 990, 995 (8th Cir. 1999);
(prosecutor's closing remarks on evidence not provided by defense improper comment on defendant's decision not to testify because only had requisite information).

United States-V-Cormier, 469 F.3d 63, 73-74 (1st Cir. 2006);
(prosecutor's remark that organic impairment of brain may not be based on psychological tests if it is not shown by physical examination improper expression of expert knowledge).

United States-V-Martin, 777 F.3d 984, 995 (8th Cir. 2015);
(the fifth amendment forbids direct comment by the government on a defendant's failure to testify or any indirect references to if it motivates by an "intent to call attention to a defendant's failure to testify or would be naturally and necessarily taken by a jury as a comment on the defendant's failure to testify").

United States-V-Inzunza, 638 F.3d 1006, 1022 (9th Cir. 2011);
(prosecutor's statement "[s]ay it isn't so" improper because it was a comment on the failure to testify).

Bucket-V-Mullin, 306 F.3d 982, 989 (10th Cir. 2002);
(prosecutor's asking witness whether defendant was trying to hide information by not testifying improper).

Marsdon-V-Moore, 847 F.2d 1536, 1547-48 (11th Cir. 1988);
(prosecutor's comment on defendant's failure to testify at his trial improper).

Rammonds-V-Commissioner Alabama Department of Corrections, 822 F.3d 1201, 1205 (11th Cir. 2016);
(prosecutor's comment "[l]et him testify" violates petitioner's Fifth Amendment rights).

United States-V-Wilchcombe, 838 F.3d 1179, 1194 (11th Cir. 2016);
(prosecutor's comments "had the two men not been involved in the drug smuggling venture, they would have said something to the Coast Guard" violated

the 5th amendment).

United States-V-Brown, 508 F.3d 1066, 1072 (D.C. Cir. 2007);

(prosecutor's remark that "[d]efendant's intent is unquestioned in this case" improper comments on defendant's decision not to testify because only defendant could refute the statement).

CHAPTER: 10

IT IS IMPROPER TO COMMENT ON A DEFENDANT'S PRIOR CONVICTIONS OR GUILTY PLEAS

CASES:

United States-V-Dworken, 855 F.2d 12, 31 (1st Cir. 1988);
(prosecutor's comment as to co-defendant's plea by saying defendant "was like all other co-defendants in this case" improper).

United States-V-Colon, 880 F.2d 650, 661 (2nd Cir. 1989);
(prosecutor's comment to defendant's prior involvement in heroin sales improper).

V.I.-V-Castillo, 550 F.2d 850, 853 (3rd Cir. 1977);
(prosecutor's comment regarding defendant's prior conviction improper).

V.I.-V-Mujahid, 990 F.2d 111, 115-16 (3rd Cir. 1993);
(prosecutor's comment in opening statement to co-defendant's guilty plea improper absent curative instruction).

United States-V-Mitchell, 1 F.3d 235, 240 (4th Cir. 1993);
(prosecutor's statement that defendants had been convicted for participating in same conspiracy improper).

United States-V-Blevins, 960 F.2d 1252, 1261 (4th Cir. 1992);
(prosecutor's comment to "defendants that plead guilty" improper absent curative instruction).

United States-V-Jackson, 339 F.3d 349, 357 (5th Cir. 2003);
(prosecutor's indirect comment to defendant's prior conviction improper because probative value substantially outweighed by undue prejudice).

United States-V-Rice, 507 F.3d 133, 140 (5th Cir. 2010);
(prosecutor's reference to defendant's previous robbery convictions improper because court prohibited their use for purpose of identification).

DePew-V-Anderson, 311 F.3d 742, 749 (6th Cir. 2002);
(prosecutor's statement, with no factual basis, that defendant previously involved in unrelated knife fight improper because referred to previous bad acts).

United States-V-McConnor, 530 F.3d 484, 500-01 (6th Cir. 2008);
(prosecutor's reference to defendant's prior drug conviction improper because violated court order prohibiting reference to defendant's prior conviction).

United States-V-Caraway, 108 F.3d 745, 761 (7th Cir. 1997);
(prosecutor's comment during opening statement that majority of individuals named in indictment had decided to plead guilty improper in absence of curative instruction).

United States-V-Richards, 719 F.3d 746, 766 (7th Cir. 2013);
(prosecutor's reference to defendant's drug related phone calls improper because created inference of propensity to deal drugs).

United States-V-Vallie, 284 F.3d 917, 921-22 (8th Cir. 2002);
(prosecutor's question to defendant concerning prior, unrelated offense improper).

Le-V-Mullin, 311 F.3d 1002, 1021 (10th Cir. 2002);
(prosecutor's implication that defendant had murdered before improper because prosecution did not show by clear and convincing evidence that prior crime occurred).

United States-V-Baker, 432 F.3d 1189, 1230 (11th Cir. 2005);
(prosecutor's comment to defendant's prior manslaughter conviction during witness cross-examination improper).

United States-V-Keen, 676 F.3d 981, 993 (11th Cir. 2012);
(prosecutor's presentation of recording that included statement that defendant had spent two (2) years in jail for "buying votes" improper introduction of prejudicial evidence or prior conviction).

United States-V-Becton, 501 F.3d 981, 995 (D.C. Cir. 2010);
(prosecutor's reference to defendant's previous incarceration improper because it constituted a statement of fact not supported by proper evidence).

CHAPTER: 11

IT IS IMPROPER FOR A PROSECUTOR TO COMMENT ON THE BAD ACTS OF THE DEFENDANT'S CODEFENDANTS AT ANY TIME

CASES:

United States-V-Dworken, 855 F.2d 12, 31 (1st Cir. 1988);
(prosecutor's reference to codefendant's guilty plea by saying defendant "was like all of the other [codefendants] in this case" improper absent curative instruction).

V.I.-V-Castillo, 550 F.2d 850, 853 (3rd Cir. 1977);
(prosecutor's comments regarding codefendant's prior felony conviction improper because it was of no concern to jury).

United States-V-Mitchell, 1 F.3d 235, 240 (4th Cir. 1993);
(prosecutor's statement that brother had been convicted for participating in some conspiracy improper because irrelevant to whether defendant should be convicted).

United States-V-Cobleigh, 75 F.3d 242, 247 (6th Cir. 1996);
(prosecutor's reference to codefendant's guilty of plea improper).

United States-V-Carraway, 108 F.3d 745, 761 (7th Cir. 1997);
(prosecutor's comment during opening statement that majority of defendants had decided to plead guilty improper absent curative instruction).

CHAPTER: 12

IT IS IMPROPER FOR A PROSECUTOR TO MAKE COMMENTS WHILE QUESTIONING THE DEFENDANT'S COCONSPIRATORS ON ANY BAD ACTS REGARDING THE DEFENDANT

CASES:

United States-V-Colon, 880 F.2d 650, 661 (2nd Cir. 1989);
(prosecutor's comment defendant's involvement in heroin sales improper because referred to past bad acts).

United States-V-Mitchell, 1 F.3d 235, 240 (4th Cir. 1993);
(prosecutor's statement that defendant's brother had been convinced for participating in same conspiracy improper because irrelevant to whether defendant should be convicted).

United States-V-Anderson, 755 F.3d 782, 796-98 (5th Cir. 2014);
(prosecutor's statement referring to coconspirator's state court conviction during rebuttal improper because unsupported by evidence admitted in trail.

DePew-V-Anderson, 311 F.3d 742, 749 (6th Cir. 2002);
(prosecutor's statement with no factual basis, that defendant previously involved in unrelated knife improper because referred to previous bad acts).

United States-V-Pedigo, 12 F.3d 618, 627 (7th Cir. 1993);
(prosecutor's remark congratulating witness for helping convict all the members of conspiracy improper because a reference to coconspirators convictions).

United States-V-Conner, 583 F.3d 1011, 1019-21 (7th Cir. 2009);
(prosecutor's introduction of defendant's previous drug deals improper because not related to charged crime).

United States-V-Vallie, 284 F.3d 917, 921-22 (8th Cir. 2002);
(prosecutor's question about defendant's prior offense improper because not related to charged crime).

Le-V-Mullin, 311 F.3d 1002, 1021 (10th Cir. 2002);
(prosecutor's implication that defendant had murdered before improper because prosecution did not show by clear and convincing evidence that prior crime occurred).

United States-V-John, 734 F.2d 657, 666 (11th Cir. 1984);
(prosecutor's remark telling jury that defendant would not have wanted coconspirators to testify improper because it forced defendant to explain coconspirator's absence by telling jury that coconspirator was a fugitive, which was an inadmissible piece of evidence).

CHAPTER: 13

IT IS IMPROPER FOR A PROSECUTOR TO VOUCH FOR THE CREDIBILITY OF HIS WITNESS

STANDARD OF REVIEW:

United States-V-Young, 470 U.S. 1, 18-19 (1985);

("the prosecutor's vouching for the credibility of witnesses… carries with it the imprimatur of the government and may induce the jury to trust the government's judgment rather than its own view of the evidence").

CASES:

United States-V-Martinez-Medina, 279 F.3d 105, 119 (1st Cir. 2002);

(prosecutor's statement vouching for testimony of four [4] cooperating witnesses improper).

United States-V-Landry, 631 F.3d 597, 606 (1st Cir. 2011);

(prosecutor's reference to getting "the right person" improper because bolstering of government's expert witness).

United States-V-Rojas, 758 F.3d 61, 64 (1st Cir. 2014);

(prosecutor's statement to the jury, "if you have any issues with the way this investigation was run, blame me. I'm responsible," improper vouching of government witness because statement in effect claims that any flaw in investigation was not probative of witness's credibility).

United States-V-Dimasi & McDonald, 817 F.Supp.2d 9, 23-24 (Dist. Mass. 2011);

(it was improper for the prosecution to tell the juror they have to face their families after the case and do not find that the case is just politics and lobbying as usual improper, but attorney helped government clean up error).

United States-V-Walker, 529 F.3d 493, 498-99 (2nd Cir. 2008);

(it was improper for the prosecutor to vouch for the credibility of government witnesses and to express his belief in the defendant's guild)(Attorney failed to object and preserve error).

United States-V-Spinelli, 551 F.3d 159, 168-70 (2nd Cir. 2008);

(prosecutor's statement that none of the witnesses had ever falsely testified improper).

United States-V-Nicole-Dunn, 753 F.3d 72, 96-97 (2nd Cir. 2014);

(prosecutor's comments in the government's opening statement repeatedly bolstered the credibility of key government witnesses, in direct contravention of related admonitions from the district court).

Jackson-V-Conway, 763 F.3d 115, 141-42 (2nd Cir. 2014);

(prosecutor violated defendant's right to due process when she mischaracterized the evidence which vouched for the credibility of the complainant).

Marshall-V-Hendricks, 307 F.3d 36, 65 (3rd Cir. 2002);
(prosecutor's statement that government witness telling truth improper).
United States-V-Lee, 612 F.3d 170, 195 (3rd Cir. 2010);
(prosecutor's story about personal experience with beagles and bird dogs improper because bolstering evidence about police dogs).
United States-V-Perez-Ruiz, 353 F.3d 1, 13 (1st Cir. 2003);
("although the prosecution's success often depends on inability to convince the jury of a particular witnesses credibility, it cannot entice the jury to find guilt on the basis of a [government] agents witness veracity").
United States-V-Vasquez-Botet, 532 F.3d 37, 53 (1st Cir. 2008);
(a prosecutor may not vouch for the credibility of one of her witnesses by making personal assurance about him; she likewise may not accomplish this goal by putting on another government witness, such as FBI agents, to make such assurance. This practice is prohibited because of its potential to snore up a witness's credibility by putting the prestige of the United States behind him and thereby inviting the jury to find guilt on some basis other than the evidence presented at trial).
Girts-V-Yanai, 501 F.3d 743, 759 (6th Cir. 2007);
(improper when the prosecutor told the jury that petitioner was the "only one person" who could explain his wife's death).
United States-V-Loaza, 107 F.3d 257, 261 (4th Cir. 1997);
(prosecutor's statement that government witnesses telling truth improper).
United States-V-Ramirez-Velasquez, 322 F.3d 868, 873-75 (5th Cir. 2003);
(prosecutor's closing remarks about reliability of witnesses in response to defense attack improper because exceeded reasonable response).
United States-V-Martinez-Laraga, 517 F.3d 258, 271 (5th Cir. 2008);
(a prosecutor should not invoke the sanction of the government as a basis for convicting a defendant)(Citing **United States-V-Ramirez-Velasquez**, 322 F.3d 868, 873-75 (5th Cir. 2003)(quoting **United States-V-Gallardo-Trapero**, 185 F.3d 307, 320 (5th Cir. 1999)).
United States-V-Meddoza, 522 F.3d 482, 498 (5th Cir. 2008);
(comment on Mendoza's clam demeanor at the border was inactive of lack of guilty knowledge improper)(J. DeMoss Dissenting).
United States-V-Gracia, 522 F.3d 597, 601 (5th Cir. 2008);
("the prosecutor should not express his or her personal belief or opinion as to the truth or falsity of any testimony or evidence or guilt of the defendant")(Citing ABA standard for prosecutors).
United States-V-Aguilar, 645 F.3d 319, 324 (5th Cir. 2011);

(prosecutor made an improper emotional appeal by stating that the agents risked their lives for "us and our children" and that it was a "sad deal" for them to be called liars. A new trial was warranted).

Hodge-V-Hurley, 426 F.3d 368, 378 (6th Cir. 2005);
(prosecutor's statement that witness absolutely believable improper).

United States-V-Henry, 545 F.3d 367, 379-80 (6th Cir. 2008);
(prosecutor's statement that witness testimony "highly believable" improper).

United States-V-Warshak, 631 F.3d 266, 301 (6th Cir. 2010);
(prosecutor's vouched for the "honest and integrity" of the prosecution team improper).

Wogen-Stahi-V-Mitchell, 668 F.3d 307, 328-29 (6th Cir. 2012);
(the prosecutor stated that the jury should believe Wheeler "[b]ecause he was telling the truth" improper).

United States-V-Cornett, 232 F.3d 570, 575 (7th Cir. 2000);
(prosecutor's statement that police witnesses "take an oath to follow the law" improper because comment vouched for witnesses good faith).

United States-V-Adams, 628 F.3d 407, 418 (7th Cir. 2010);
(prosecutor's statement that government witness took an oath to tell the truth and that prosecutor believed that she told truth improper).

Jordan-V-Hepp, 831 F.3d 837, 848-49 (7th Cir. 2016);
("this is a text book of improper vouching. The prosecutor engaged in one of the forms of argumentation that the Supreme Court repeatedly has identified as improper, implying that the jury should believe a witness based on evidence not presented to the jury").

Garrison-V-Burt, 707 F.Supp.2d 945, 936 (U.S. Dist. Iowa 2010);
(prosecutor made improper remarks during opening arguments, reasonably believing that Martin's testimony would establish personal knowledge of Garrison's Oxycontin Sale)(But no intent found).

United States-V-Bass, 708 F.Supp.2d 931, 937 (U.S. Dist. Neb. 2010);
(improper for prosecutor to vouch for the credibility of his witnesses truthfulness).

Close-V-United States, 679 F.3d 714, 717 (8th Cir. 2012);
(prosecutor's comments that police witness was a sworn police officer for 17 years, had no motive to lie, and would lose his job if he lied improper comment on government witness credibility).

United States-V-Weatherspoon, 410 F.3d 1142, 1146 (9th Cir. 2005);
(prosecutor's statement witness had no reason to lie improper).

Sechrest-V-Ignacio, 549 F.3d 789, 811 (9th Cir. 2008);

(by vouching for the truthfulness of his own unsorted, inaccurate assertions, the prosecutor committed flagrant misconduct).

United States-V-Combs, 379 F.3d 584, 573 (9th Cir. 2004);
(improper for the prosecutor to ask the defendant if the agent had lied on the stand).

United States-V-Younger, 398 F.3d 1179, 1191 (9th Cir. 2005);
(we do not condone the prosectuor's argument, because of 'we know' readily blurs the line between improper vouching and legitimate summary).

Hein-V-Sullivan, 601 F.3d 897, 913 (9th Cir. 2010);
(prosecutor's description of witness as "very powerful and credible" improper).

United States-V-Comett, 232 F.3d 570, 575-76 (7th Cir. 2000);
(prosecutor's statement that "police offers take oath to follow the law" improper).

United States-V-Moore, 651 F.3d 30, 61-62 (D.C. Cir. 2011);
(overview testimony of FBI agent improper, but harmless do to overwhelming evidence).

United States-V-Alexander, 741 F.3d 866, 870 (7th Circ. 2014);
(improper for prosecutor to argue that officer Monzel would not violate his oath or break the law)(Harmless error).

United States-V-Barlow, 444 F.3d 1255, 1266 (10th Cir. 2006);
(prosecutor's vouching for witnesses by implying judge approved their credibility improper).

United States-V-McCann, 613 F.3d 486, 496 (10th Cir. 2010);
(improper for the prosecutor to vouch for the credibility of police officers)(error counterbalanced by defense counsel's improper remarks I.D. at 498).

Parker-V-Allen, 565 F.3d 1256, 1273 (11th Cir. 2009);
("[w]e vouch for the credibility of those witnesses by putting them on the stand and I submit to you that they've told the truth" improper).

United States-V-Reed, 522 F.3d 354, 360 N.6 (D.C. Cir. 2008);
(prosecutor's rhetorical question if agent would risk career by falsely testifying improper).

CHAPTER: 14

IT IS IMPROPER FOR A PROSECUTOR TO PROSECUTE FOR VINDICTIVE REASONS

STANDARD OF REVIEW:

Blackledge-V-Perry, 417 U.S. 21, 31, 94 S.CT. 2098, 40 L.ED.2d 628 (1974);
(Holding: that vindictive prosecution could contravene due process and justify bar to retrial).

North Carolina-V-Pearce, 395 U.S. 711, 89 S.CT. 2072, 23 L.ED.2d 604 (1969);
(Held: that the Fourteenth Amendment was applicable to the States and forbids multiple punishment for the same offense)(This is perhaps the first case, to recognize prosecutorial vindictiveness).

CASES:

North Carolina-V-Pearce, 395 U.S. 711, 89 S.CT. 2072, 23 L.ED.2d 656 (1969);
(Finding a presumption of vindictiveness where as a judge imposed a more severe sentencing after a new trial).

United States-V-Goodwin, 457 U.S. 368, 372, 102 S.CT. 2485, 73 L.ED.2d 74 (1978);
("to punish a person because he had done what the law plainly allows him to do is a process violation of the most basic sort")(Citing **Bordenkircher-V-Hayes**, 434 U.S. 357, 365, 98 S.CT. 663, 54 L.ED.2d 604 (1978));

United States-V-Sanders, 211 F.3d 711, 716 (2nd Cir. 2000);
(due process violations arise if prosecutor seeks to punish defendant for exercising legal rights).

United States-V-Perry, 335 F.3d 316, 324 (4th Circ. 2003);
(noting that "a presumption of prosecutorial vindictiveness is generally warranted only in a post-conviction setting such as when a defendant successfully attacks his conviction on appeal, and then received a harsher sentence on retrial").

United States-V-Jackson, 327 F.3d 273 (4th Cir. 2003); cert. Denied, 540 U.S. 1019, 124 S.CT. L.ED.2d 434 (2003);
(if defendant is unable to demonstrate the required animus, he may still present evidence of circumstances from which improper vindictive motive may be presumed).

United States-V-Johnson, 325 F.3d 205 (4th Cir. 2003), cert. Denied, 540 U.S. 897, 124 S.CT. 257, 157 L.Ed.2d 176 (2003);
(to establish prosecutorial vindictiveness, the defendant must show through objection evidence that prosecutor acted with animus toward defendant and that defendant would not have been prosecuted but for that animus).

United States-V-Pitman, 642 F.3d 583, 586 (7th Cir. 2011);

(vindictive prosecution claim arises if prosecution pursued in retaliation for defendant's exercise of a legal right).

United States-V-LaBeau, 734 F.3d 551, 566 (6th Cir. 2013);

(presumption of vindictiveness when a defendant has established that (1) the prosecutor has some stake in deterring the defendant's exercise of his rights, and 920 the prosecutor's conduct was unreasonable).

United States-V-Stroud, 673 F.3d 854, 859 (8th Cir. 2012);

(vindictive prosecution claim arises when prosecutor punished defendant for exercising valid constitutional rights).

United States-V-Jenkins, 504 F.3d 694, 702 (9th Cir. 2007);

(vindictive prosecution where government filed additional alien smuggling charges against Jenkins).

United States-V-Kent, 649 F.3d 908, 912 (9th Cir. 2011);

(due process violated when prosecutor seeks additional charges to punish defendant for exercising constitutional or statutory rights).

United States-V-Thomas, 410 F.3d 1235, 1246 (10th Cir. 2005);

(due process violation arises if prosecutor seeks to punish defendant for exercising legal right during criminal proceedings).

United States-V-Kendrick, 682 F.3d 947, 981 (11th Cir. 2012);

(retaliatory motive for bringing new charges constitutes a due process violation).

United States-V-Safavian, 649 F.3d 688, 692 (D.C. Cir. 2011);

(prosecutor is precluded from penalizing a defendant for invoking any legally protected right during a criminal trial).

CHAPTER: 15

IT VIOLATES DUE PROCESS FOR A PROSECUTOR TO WITHHOLD EXCULPATORY EVIDENCE

STANDARD OF REVIEW:

Brady-V-Maryland, 373 U.S. 83, 83 S.CT. 1194, 10 L.ED.2d 215 (1953);
(failure to disclose favorable evidence, violates due process).
United States-V-Bagley, 473 U.S. 667, 668, 105 S.CT. 3375, 87 L.ED.2d 481 (1985);
(defendant must show a reasonable probability of a different result).
Kyles-V-Whitley, 514 U.S. 419, 441, 115 S.CT. 1555, 131 L.ED.2d 490 (1995);
(requiring a "cumulative evaluation" of the materiality of wrongfully withheld evidence).
Wearry-V-Cain, 136 S.CT. 1002, (2016);
(failed to disclose deal with informant).
CASES:
Cone-V-Bell, 556 U.S. 449, 469 (2009);
("[W]hen the State withheld from a criminal defendant evidence that is material to his guilt or punishment, it violates his right to due process of law in violation of the Fourteenth Amendment).
United States-V-Aviles-Colon, 536 F.3d 1, 20 (1st Cir. 2008);
(withheld DEA reports favorable to accused because they contradicted testimony of government witnesses).
United States-V-Skelly, 442 F.3d 94, 100 (2nd Cir. 2006);
(concluding prosecution's duty to disclose "does not extend to the knowledge of an ordinary expert witness who was not involved with investigation of the case").
United States-V-Triumph Capitol Grp. Inc., 544 F.3d 149, 162 (2nd Cir. 2008);
(FBI agent's notes favorable to an accused because they agreed with the accused's version of events).
Wilson-V-Beard, 539 F.3d 651, 660-62 (3rd Cir. 2009);
(evidence of government's history of severe mental problems favorable to an accused because it showed the witness was prescribed psychotropic drugs during the relevant time period).
Dennis-V-Philadelphia, 834 F.3d 263, 293 (3rd Cir. 2016);
(Brady violation for prosecutor failing to disclose receipt which would have impeached credibility of States witness and corroborated defense alibi).
Monroe-V-Angelone, 323 F.3d 286, 300 (4th Cir. 2003);
(undisclosed evidence favorable to accused because it could have been used to impeach government witnesses).

Owens-V-Baltimore City State's Attorney's Office, 767 F.3d 379, 397-98 (4th Cir. 2014);

(undisclosed witness's statements favorable to accused because they would have supported defense's contentions that the witness was the individual who raped and murdered the victim).

Avila-V-Quarterman, 560 F.3d 299, 307 (5th Cir. 2009);

("it is well settled that if a member of the police department has knowledge of Brady material, such knowledge is imputed to the prosecutor's").

Banks-V-Thaler, 583 F.3d 295, 311 (5th Cir. 2009);

(prosecution withheld, certain transcripts of police interviews with government witnesses favorable to the accused because they could impeach witness testimony).

Gumm-V-Mitchell, 775 F.3d 345, 370 (6th Cir. 2014);

(when the prosecutor fails to turn over numerous pieces of favorable evidence, the proper focus of Brady's materiality inquiry is on the cumulative effect of the unsupported evidence on the jury's verdict).(Brady violation for failing to disclose favorable witness statements)(other suspects).

Barton-V-Kern, 786 F.3d 450, 467-69 (6th Cir. 2015);

(state failed to disclose evidence that would have impeached states only witness).

Martinez-V-United States, 793 F.3d 533, 555 (6th Cir. 2015);

(Brady violation for failure to disclose U.S. Consular Records records related to the 2009 communications between the United States and Mexican authorities about the Oaxacan arrest warrant)(failure to disclose this document denied defendant right to file suppression motion).

United States-V-Bland, 517 F.3d 930, 934 (7th Cir. 2003);

(prosecutor withheld evidence related to an investigation into misconduct by a detective who testified favorable to an accused because this evidence would have impeached credibility of witness).

United States-V-Cazares, 465 F.3d 327, 333-34 (8th Cir. 2006);

(withheld codefendant's statement favorable to an accused because relevant to defendant's role in conspiracy and related to expert testimony presented by government).

United States-V-Gamez-Orduna, 235 F.3d 453, 461 (9th Cir. 2000);

("the suppression of material evidence helpful to the accused, whether at trial or an a motion to suppress, violates due process").

Mike-V-Ryan, 711 F.3d 998, 1012-13 (9th Cir. 2018);

(policeman's long history of misconduct and lying under oath was favorable to defendant because it impeached his testimony to defendant's confession).

United States-V-Sedaghty, 728 F.3d 885, 900 (9th Cir. 2013);

("in evaluating materiality, we focus on whether the withholding of the evidence undermined our trust in the fairness of the trial and the resulting verdict").

Comstock-V-Humphries, 786 F.3d 701 (9th Cir. 2015);

(failure to disclose witnesses inconsistent statements in violation of Brady).

Nuckols-V-Gibson, 233 F.3d 1261, 1266 (10th Cir. 2000);

(finding a Brady violation where prosecution withheld evidence that was material to whether the defendant's confession should have been suppressed).

Gonzales-V-McKune, 247 F.3d 1066, 1077 (10th Cir. 2001);

(information about the lack of sperm in semen sample collected exonerate victim was exculpatory even though it did not conclusively exonerate defendant who did not have low sperm count).

United States-V-Ford, 550 F.3d 975, 982-83 (10th Cir. 2008);

(undisclosed additional emails favorable to accused because defendant's entrapment defense was based on frequency of undercover agent's solicitation).

McCormick-V-Parker, 821 F.3d 1240 (10th Cir. 2016);

(Brady violation when State failed to disclose their expert witnesses expired credentials, which violated his due process rights).

United States-V-Johnson, 592 F.3d 164, 172 (D.C. Cir. 2010);

(information that defendant's cousin owned seized heroin should have been disclosed because favorable to defendant, States theory was that heroin belonged to defendant).

United States-V-Pasha, 797 F.3d 1122, 1138 (D.C. Cir. 2015);

(had witnesses prior statements been disclosed, it would have created a reasonable probability of a different outcome, as to defendant's guilt).

Boyette-V-Lefevre, 246 F.3d 76, 92-93 (2nd Cir. 2001);

(Brady violation because cumulative effect of fire marshal's report cast doubt on main prosecution witness's ability to immediately recognize defendant on sight).

Monroe-V-Angelone, 323 F.3d 286, 315-17 (4th Cir. 2003);

(Brady violation because cumulative effect of plea deals and inconsistent statements could have undermined prosecution's proof of premeditation and malice for first degree murder charge).

Mahler-V-Kaylo, 537 F.3d 494, 503-04 (5th Cir. 2008);

(Brady violation because pretrial witnesses statements about details of struggle taken collectively could have been used to impeach key eyewitness).

Jells-V-Mitchell, 538 F.3d 478, 506-07 (6th Cir. 2008);

(Brady violation because withheld statements of friend of victim, victim's sister, victim's boyfriend, and police undermined prosecution assertion of kidnapping).

Gody-V-Basinger, 604 F.3d 394, 401-02 (7th Cir. 2010);

(Brady violation because cumulative effect of inconsistencies in witness testimony and confession by someone other than defendant material to the outcome of the case).

United States-V-O'Conner, 64 F.3d 355, 359-60 (8th Cir. 1995);

(Brady violation because undisclosed threats to government witness, undisclosed interview reports, and undisclosed efforts by conspirators to influence witness testimony during trial cumulatively undermined confidence in credibility of sole witnesses against defendant).

Valdovinos-V-McGrath, 598 F.3d 586, 579 (9th Cir. 2010);

(Brady violation because cumulative effect of undermined evidence, against backdrop of relatively weak prosecution case, undermined confidence in verdict).

Trammell-V-McKune, 485 F.3d 546, 551 (10th Cir. 2007);

(Brady violation because cumulative impact of suppressed receipts would have bolstered defendant's theory of the case).

United States-V-Loyd, 71 F.3d 408, 413 (D.C. Cir. 1995);

(Brady violation because cumulative effect of undisclosed tax return undermined confidence in the verdict).

Fuentes-V-Griffen, 829 F.3d 233, 240-41 (2nd Cir. 2016);

(prosecutor failed to disclose mental health records of key witness, in violation of Brady).

a. BRADY VIOLATION FOR FAILING TO DISCLOSE DEAL TO TESTIFY:

STANDARD OF REVIEW:

Giglio-V-United States, 405 F.3d 150, 154, 92 S.CT. 763, 31 L.ED.2d 104 (1972);

(reversing a conviction where the government failed to disclose that it had granted immunity to a witness upon whose testimony the government's case was heavily dependent).

Smith-V-Cain, 152 S.CT. 627, 630 (2012);

(police officer's undisclosed statements that contradicted his testimony material where the officer's testimony was the only evidence linking the defendant to the crime).

CASES:

Outmette-V-Moran, 942 F.2d 1, 10-11 (1st Cir. 1992);

(Brady violation where attorney failed to disclose voluminous convictions of and prosecution deals made with prosecution's main witnesses against defendant).

United States-V-Duval, 496 F.3d 64, 73 (1st Cir. 2007);

(Brady violation for failing to disclose to the defense in a timely manner that confidential informants had been paid)(No prejudice).

United States-V-Flores-Rivera, 787 F.3d 1, 20-21 (1st Cir. 2015);

(undisclosed evidence that attacked the witness's motivation in his testimony was material because the predominant prosecutorial evidence in the case consisted of witnesses testimony).

Drumgold-V-Callahan, 707 F.3d 28, 41-42 (1st Cir. 2018);

(Brady violation where prosecution failed to disclose that police arranged free housing for witness).

Monroe-V-Angelone, 323 F.3d 286, 314 (4th Cir. 2003);

(Brady violation where government failed to reveal leniency agreement with key witness and prosecution explicitly stressed absence of such deals in closing statement).

LaCaze-V-Warden, La Corr. Inst. For Women, 645 F.3d 728, 736-38 (5th Cir. 2011);

(Brady violation where Government failed to disclose promise not to prosecute coconspirator's son because coconspirator's testimony was only evidence of defendant's intent).

United States-V-Mills, 592 F.3d 730, 735 (6th Cir. 2010);

(Brady violation where government failed to disclose paid confidential informant status of witness who provided only evidence contradicted defendant's self-defense claim).

United States-V-Boyd, 55 F.3d 239, 245-46 (7th Cir. 1995);

(Brady violation where government failed to disclosed favors done for witnesses, vacated on other grounds 531 U.S. 1135 (2001).

Reutter-V-Solem, 888 F.2d 578, 581-82 (8th Cir. 1989);

(Brady violation where, even absent express deal between prosecution and critical witness, prosecution failed to disclose that witness was a candidate for communication of sentence).

Phillip-V-Ornaski, 673 F.3d 1158, 1187-88 (9th Cir. 2012);

(Brady violation where government failed to disclose plea offer extended to but not accepted by coconspirator in exchange for testimony).

Horton-V-Mayle, 408 F.3d 570, 581 (9th Cir. 2004);

(Brady violation for failing to disclose deal of leniency with states key witnesses).

Douglas-V-Workman, 560 F.3d 1156, 1174-76 (10th Cir. 2009);
(Brady violation where government failed to disclose deal struck between state and sole witness linking defendant to the murder).

United States-V-Arnold, 117 F.3d 1308, 1315-16 (11th Cir. 1991);
(Brady violation where government failed to disclose audio recordings of conversations between important witness and IRS officer where witness's expectation of favorable treatment was apparent contradicting witness's trial testimony that he did not expect any favorable treatment).

United States-V-Ignasiak, 567 F.3d 1217, 1237-39 (11th Cir. 2012);
(Brady violation where government failed to disclose records of its expert's prior criminal activity and large compensation for his testimony).

United States-V-Smith, 77 F.3d 511, 516 (D.C. Cir. 1996);
(Brady violation where government failed to disclose deal to dismiss charges against key witness who claimed to be testifying because he wanted a fresh start).

a. BRADY VIOLATION & GUILTY PLEAS:

STANDARD OF REVIEW:

United States-V-Ruiz, 536 F.3d 622, 629-33 (2002);
(no Brady violation where government required defendant to waive access to impeachment evidence prior to entering into plea agreement).

CASES:

Ferrara-V-United States, 456 F.3d 278, 297 (1st Cir. 2006);
(the sad fact is that the government promised the petitioner that it would carry out fully its obligation to produce exculpatory evidence but instead manipulated a key witness, deliberately chose not to reveal to the petitioner the stunning evidence concerning Jordan's recantation, yet presented falsely to the petitioner that it had kept its promise. This was impermissible conduct. The district court supportably found that, absent this conduct, there was a reasonable probability that the petitioner would not have plead guilty but, rather, would have rejected the proffered pea agreement and opted for a trial. Ferrera, 384 F.Supp.2d at 430. Given the totality of the circumstances and the district courts credibility calls, we are constrained to conclude that the petitioner's plea was constitutionally infirm under the rule announced in Brady-V-Maryland, infra, petitioner is entitled to relief).

United States-V-Avellino, 136 F.3d 249, 255-58 (2nd Cir. 1993);
(knowing and voluntary guilty plea subject to challenge if Brady violation occurs, government's obligation to disclose Brady material is pertinent to determination of whether or not to plead guilty).

McCann-V-Mangialardi, 337 F.3d 782, 788 (7th Cir. 2003);

(voluntariness or guilty plea can be challenged on Brady grounds if government withholds evidence of factual innocence).

White-V-United States, 858 F.2d 416, 422 (8th Cir. 1989);

(voluntariness of guilty plea challenged on Brady Grounds).

United States-V-Wright, 43 F.3d 491, 496 (10th Cir. 1994);

(under limited circumstances, Brady violation can render defendant's guilty plea involuntary).

CHAPTER: 16

IT VIOLATES DUE PROCESS FOR A PROSECUTOR TO DESTROY EXCULPATORY EVIDENCE

STANDARD OF REVIEW:

Arizona-V-Youngblood, 488 U.S. 51, 53 (1988);
(A petitioner may be entitled to relief if he can show that the government destroyed exculpatory evidence in bad faith).

CASES:

United States-V-Hughes, 211 F.3d 676, 689 (1st Cir. 2000);
(government not liable for missing photos of crime scene because FBI repeatedly requested photos under control of Mexican officials).

Illinois-V-Fisher, 540 U.S. 544, 547, 124 S.CT. 1200, 1202, 157 L.ED.2d 1060 (2004);
(unpreserved evidence was potentially useful because the defense could have subjected it to a Fifth Test).

Yarris-V-County of Delaware, 465 F.3d 129, 142-43 (3rd Cir. 2006);
(bad faith where government left DNA evidence it knew to be exculpatory in a paper bag under a detective desk, destroying the evidence).

United States-V-Moore, 452 F.3d 382, 388 (5th Cir. 2006);
("impeachable withheld evidence must be either (1) material and exculpatory or (2) only potentially useful, in combination of bad faith on the part of the government").

United States-V-Wright, 260 F.3d 588, 571 (6th Cir. 2001);
("the destruction of material exculpatory evidence violates due process regardless of whether acted in bad faith").

United States-V-Cooper, 983 F.2d 928, 931 (9th Cir. 1993);
(due process violated when government destroyed laboratory equipment allegedly used by defendant to manufacture methamphetamine because equipment's possible exculpatory value apparent after repeated suggestions to government agents that such equipment could not withstand high temperatures required to make methamphetamine).

United States-V-Estrada, 453 F.3d 1208, 1212-13 (9th Cir. 2006);
(only requiring a showing of bad faith when the evidence is "potentially exculpatory, as opposed to apparently exculpatory).

United States-V-Yap, 852 F.2d 1249, 1256 (10th Cir. 1988);
(government not liable for destruction of business records that were returned to third parties before defendant committed crime).

United States-V-Bohl, 852 F.2d 1249, 1256 (10th Cir. 1988);
(due process violation when government destroyed radio tower legs because of evidence of Tower's unique chemical composition could have aided defense's

case and defense requested information about legs before they were destroyed).

Bullock-V-Carver, 297 F.3d 1036, 1056 (10th Cir. 2002);

("a defendant can obtain relief under the due process clause when he can show that a police department destroyed evidence with an exculpatory value that was apparent before [it] was destroyed... Where, however, the police only failed to preserve potentially useful evidence that might have been exculpatory, a defendant must prove that the police acted in bad faith by destroying the evidence.") (internal citation omitted).

CHAPTER: 17

IT VIOLATES DUE PROCESS FOR A PROSECUTOR TO BREACH A PLEA AGREEMENT

STANDARD OF REVIEW:

Puckett-V-United States, 656 U.S. 129, 137 (2009);
(stating "plea agreements are essentially contracts").
Blackledge-V-Allison, 431 U.S. 63, 76, 80-82 (1977);
(allegations of breach entitles defendant to evidentiary hearing unless defendant's allegations are "palpably incredible" or patently frivolous or false").
CASES:
Demis-V-United States, 30 F.3d 220, 222-23 (1st Cir. 1994);
(defendant entitles to further proceedings to determine whether government breached promise to put defendant in witness protection).
United States-Gonczy, 357 F.3d 50, 54 (1st Cir. 2004);
(government breached promise to recommend sentence of 70 months by explicitly asking for 70 months out implicitly arguing for higher sentence).
United States-V-Griffen, 510 F.3d 354, 364-65 (2nd Cir. 2007);
(government breached plea agreement by, without solicitation, informing court it questioned whether defendant truly accepted responsibility despite agreement barring government from opposing adjustments for acceptance of responsibility).
United States-V-Hodge, 412 F.3d 479, 487 (3rd Cir. 2005);
(government breached plea agreement to refrain from making sentencing recommendation by implying at sentencing that defendant should not be released into community).
United States-V-Lewis, 633 F.3d 262, 270-71 (4th Cir. 2011);
(government breached plea agreement by failing to correct court's misunderstanding of the concurrent sentencing provision).
United States-V-Harper, 643 F.3d 135, 143 (5th Cir. 2011);
(government breached plea agreement by using defendant's immunized statements to advocate higher sentencing range even though plea agreement recognizing that government would "make available" all evidence to court).
United States-V-Chavful, 781 F.3d 758, 762-64 (5th Cir. 2015);
(government breached plea agreement by using information provided by defendant to increase sentencing contrary to protection in plea agreement).
United States-V-Harris, 473 F.3d 222, 225-26 (6th Cir. 2006);
(government breached plea agreement when prosecutor mistakenly recommended probation, but failed to debrief defendant because agreement mandated debriefing).
United States-V-Keller, 665 F.3d 711, 714 (6th Cir. 2011);
(government breached plea agreement by arguing for sentencing greater than

guideline range when agreement mandated recommendation at high end of sentencing guideline).

United States-V-Diaz-Jimenez, 622 F.3d 692, 696 (7th Cir. 2010); (government breached plea agreement when prosecutor mistakenly recommended sentence at top of guidelines range and did not unequivocally retract recommendation).

United States-V-Mosely, 505 F.3d 804, 808 (8th Cir. 2007); (government breached agreement by arguing that defendant failed to accept responsibility).

United States-V-Lewis, 673 F.3d 758, 762 (8th Cir. 2011); (government breached plea agreement by denying defendant's right to participate in sentencing nearing plea agreement's plain language gave defendant right to participate in "any proceeding related to this case").

United States-V-Whitley, 673 F.3d 956, 971 & n.4 (9th Cir. 2012); (government breached plea agreement by arguing that a base offense implicitly arguing for sentence greater than the terms of agreement).

United States-V-Manzo, 675 F.3d 1204, 1211-12 (9th Cir. 2012); (government breached plea agreement by arguing that a base offense level of 3d was correct when agreement stated government would recommend base offense level of 34).

United States-V-Heredia, 768 F.3d 1220, 1232-34 (9th Cir. 2014); (government breached plea agreement by implicitly arguing for increased sentence through inflammatory references to defendant's criminal history contrary to promise in agreement not to argue for increased sentence).

United States-V-Villa-Vasquez, 536 F.3d 1189, 1197 (10th Cir. 2008); (government breached plea agreement by encouraging upward departure because it promised to recommend "low-end guideline sentence").

United States-V-Mendoza, 698 F.3d 1303, 1309-10 (10th Cir. 2012); (government breached plea agreement by failing to keep promise to recommend sentence at low end guideline range).

United States-V-De La Garza, 516 F.3d 1266, 1270 (11th Cir. 2008); (government breached plea agreement by challenging veracity of facts stipulated to in plea agreement).

United States-V-Wolf, 127 F.3d 84, 86 (D.C. Cir. 1997); (government breached plea agreement by failing to ask sentencing judge to award defendant "full credit acceptance of responsibility").

CHAPTER: 18

IT IS IMPROPER CONDUCT FOR A PROSECUTOR TO USE HIS OWN OFFICE TO SUPPORT HIS CREDIBILITY TO PROSECUTE A CASE

CASES:

Floyd-V-Meachum, 907 F.2d 347, 354-55 (2nd Cir. 1990);
(prosecutor's request that jury consider prosecutor's own integrity and ethics before deliberating on evidence improper).

United States-V-Gallardo-Trapero, 185 F.3d 307, 319 (5th Cir. 1999);
(prosecutor's closing argument asking whether federal agents and prosecutor would "risk their career" to commit perjury improper).

United States-V-Warshak, 631 F.3d 266, 303 (6th Cir. 2010);
(prosecutor's statement about his military service and his quasi-famous colleague improper because only served to enhance prosecutor's "stature in the eyes of the jury").

United States-V-Cornett, 232 F.3d 570, 573 (7th Cir. 2000);
(prosecutor's statement that prosecutors take oaths and don't "stick people with charges" improper invocation of oath to bolster his own witness's credibility).

Copeland-V-Washington, 232 F.3d 969, 975 (8th Cir. 2000);
(prosecutor's comparison of his own traditional marriage with defendant's marriage improper).

United States-V-Fredrick, 78 F.3d 1370, 1380 (9th Cir. 1996);
(prosecutor's comments portraying himself as ally of court improper).

Cargle-V-Mullin, 317 F.3d 1196, 1218 (10th Cir. 2003);
(prosecutor's remark that state does not prosecute innocent people improper).

Cargill-V-Turpin, 120 F.3d 1366, 1385 (11th Cir. 1997);
(prosecutor's statement chat "so seldom do we see crimes so cold-blooded and not [1] but [2] bullets fired into the heads" improper because invokes expertise of prosecutor as to whether this particular crime deserved death penalty).

CHAPTER: 19

IT IS IMPROPER FOR A PROSECUTOR TO TESTIFY AT THE TRIAL HE IS PROSECUTING

CASES:

Riddle-V-Cockrell, 288 F.3d 713, 721 (5th Cir. 2002);
(a prosecutor may not testify at the trial he is prosecuting. It is frowned upon by the courts and creates an unfair trail).

CHAPTER: 20

IT IS IMPROPER CONDUCT FOR A PROSECUTOR TO ASK THE JURY TO ACT AS A CONSCIENCE FOR THE COMMUNITY, OR MAKE OTHER REMARKS THAT ARE LIKELY TO INFLAME THE JURY'S PASSION AGAINST THE DEFENDANT AND CAUSE THEM TO CONVICT FOR REASONS OTHER THAN GUILT

CASES:

United States-V-Santos-Rivera, 726 F.3d 17, 27 (1st Cir. 2013);
(prosecutor's taking gun from the evidence table and brandishing it before the jury was improper because "obviously inflammatory" and unnecessary).

United States-V-Mooney, 315 F.3d 54, 59 (1st Cir. 2002);
(prosecutor's remarks during opening statement contrasting jurors sense of safety in community with armed robbery improperly appealed to the jury to act in ways other than dispassionate arbiters of the facts, but no prejudiced because jury instruction addressed remarks and evidence of guilt over-whelming).

United States-V-De La Paz-Rentas, 613 F.3d 18, 26 (1st Cir. 2010);
(prosecutor's argument that jury should "do [its] duty" improper because could convey to jury that its job was to convict).

United States-V-Elias, 285 F.3d 183, 190-92 (2nd Cir. 2002);
(prosecutor's characterization of defense argument as insult to victim improper because designed to inflame jury, but no prejudice because reference was isolated incident and did not bolster strongest part of government's case).

United States-V-Berrios, 676 F.3d 118, 135 (3rd Cir. 2012);
(prosecutor's reading of commemorative poem about victim and using enlarge photo of victim's face during closing argument improper because served no purpose other than appealing to jurors emotions).

Marshall-V-Hendricks, 307 F.3d 36, 66 (3rd Cir. 2002);
(prosecutor's statement and her love for her family improper because the remark was intended to inflame jury).

United States-V-Lighty, 616 F.3d 321, 360-61 (4th Cir. 2010);
(prosecutor's statement that victim's family was asking for the death penalty improper because not supported by evidence in record and based on inadmissible victim impact evidence).

United States-V-Runyan, 707 F.3d 475, 514 (4th Cir. 2013);
(prosecutor urging the jury to "send a message to the community" improper).

Learmonthly-V-Sears-Roebuck & Co., 631 F.3d 724, 732 (5th Cir. 2011);
(plaintiff's counsel's "conscience-of-the-community" argument improper because likely to prejudice viewpoint of jury against out-of-state corporation).

Frazier-V-Huffman, 343 F.3d 780, 792-93 (6th Cir. 2003);
(prosecutor's references to character of victim during closing argument and using empty chair to represent victim improper, but no prejudice because misconduct not "centerpiece" of prosecutor's argument and judge issued instruction).

United States-V-Parkes, 668 F.3d 295, 306 (6th Cir. 2012);
(prosecutor's suggestion that acquittal would allow defendant to "keep the four million" improper because suggestion was false).

Cumm-V-Mitchell, 775 F.3d 345, 379 (6th Cir. 2014);
(prosecutor's comments painting defendant as a sexual deviant and animal killer improper and the comment was for nothing more than to "inflame the passion of the jury").

United States-V-Morgan, 113 F.3d 85, 90 (7th Cir. 1997);
(prosecutor's comment asking the jurors to place themselves in witness place and to consider how they would feel if they were called liars, and implication that an acquittal would make people less willing to come forward and testify improper because related to issue beyond guilt or innocence of defendant).

Hough-V-Anderson, 272 F.3d 878, 902-04 (7th Cir. 2001);
(prosecutor's comments to jurors during sentencing that they would deprecate seriousness of the crime if they did not impose death penalty and that they assumed power to kill when they took their oath improper).

United States-V-Mannava, 565 F.3d 412, 414 (7th Cir. 2009);
(prosecutor's incessant harping that defendant had been intending to rape a minor improper because prejudicial and not supported by evidence and undoubtedly trying to inflame the jury).

Copeland-V-Washington, 232 F.3d 959, 975 (8th Cir. 2000);
(prosecutor's evoking jury's fear or crime by comparing defendant to violent drug gangs improper).

Sinisterra-V-United States, 606 F.3d 900, 910-11 (8th Cir. 2010);
(prosecutor's comment that jury could act as "conscience of the community" and "send a message to all other drug dealers" improper).

Drayden-V-White, 232 F.3d 704, 712-13 (9th Cir. 2000);
(prosecutor's soliloquy in persona of deceased victim improper because inflamed jury's sympathy for dead man and suggested role of jury to vindicate victim rather than punish crime, but no prejudice because statements were reasonable inference from evidence).

United States-V-Sanchez, 639 F.3d 1252, 1256-57 (9th Cir. 2011);
(prosecutor's statement that an acquittal would "send a memo" to other drug couriers to use same defense improper because asked jury to consider social implications of verdict rather than guilt or innocence of defendant).

Spears-V-Mullins, 343 F.3d 1215, 1246 (10th Cir. 2003);
(prosecutor's emphasis on victims good character, in comparison to defendant's, improper, but no prejudice because remarks did not result in unfair

trial).

Wilson-V-Simmons, 536 F.3d 1064, 1120-21 (10th Cir. 2008);

(prosecutor's comments that jury would deliver justice as "greater equalizer" improper because suggested civic duty to convict).

United States-V-Anaya, 727 F.3d 1043, 1059 (10th Cir. 2013);

(prosecutor's comment that jury should be angry with defendant improper).

United States-V-McLean, 138 F.3d 1398, 1405 (11th Cir. 1998);

(prosecutor's reference during closing argument to plight of "crack-addicted babies" improper because unrelated to testimony of witnesses or defendant's culpability and blatant appeal to fears and prejudice of jurors but no prejudice because overwhelming evidence of guilt).

United States-V-McGarity, 669 F.3d 1218, 1246 (11th Cir. 2012);

(prosecutor's prompting of jurors to recognize victims in child pornography case as their own daughters and granddaughters improper appeal to jurors emotions).

United States-V-Johnson, 231 F.3d 43, 46-49 (D.C. Cir. 2000);

(prosecutor's suggestion that jury should convict defendant to protect others from drugs improper).

United States-V-Fahnbulleh, 752 F.3d 470, 479-80 (D.C. Cir. 2014);

(prosecutor's references to "taxpayers" in closing argument of prosecution of defendants for submission of false claims to USAID improper).

CHAPTER: 21

IT VIOLATES DUE PROCESS FOR A PROSECUTOR TO ALLOW A WITNESS TO TESTIFY FALSELY

STANDARD OF REVIEW:

Mooney-V-Holohan, 294 U.S. 103, 55 S. CT. 340 (1945);
(the court established the general proposition that a prosecutor's knowing and intentional use of perjured testimony in obtaining a conviction violates the defendant's due process rights, and denies him a fair trial).

Alcorta-V-Texas, 355 U.S. 28, 78 S.CT. 103 (1957);
(the court held that the prosecutor's knowing failure to correct exculpatory perjured testimony violated due process).

Napue-Y-Illinoise, 360 U.S. 264, 79 S.CT. 1173, 3 L.ED.2d 1217 (1959);
(the government "may not knowingly use false evidence" or "allow it to go uncorrected when it appears." Id. at 269).

CASES:

Mastracchio-V-Vose, 274 F.3d 590, 602 (1st Cir. 2001);
(prosecutor's failure to correct witness's false statement improper).

Shih Wei-V-Flion, 335 F.3d 119, 127-30 (2nd Cir. 2003);
(prosecutor's failure to correct government witness's false testimony and subsequent attempt to bolster witness's credibility improper and violated due process).

Drake-V-Portuondo, 553 F.3d 230, 341 (2nd Cir. 2009);
(prosecutor's knowledge that expert witness testimony   was false required reversal).

United States-V-John-Baptiste, 747 F.3d 186, 210-11 (3rd Cir. 2014);
(prosecutor's introduction of witness who had stolen another person's identity improper because government records listed two [2] individual under the witness's name and prosecution failed to investigate further).

United States-V-Bartko, 728 F.3d 327, 337 (4th Cir. 2013);
(prosecutor's failure to correct witness's false testimony that government did not make him any promises improper because government did make the witnesses promises).

United States-V-Mason, 293 F.3d 826, 829-30 (5th Cir. 2002);
(prosecutor's failure to correct government witnesses' statements regarding plea agreement improper and violated due process).

United States-V-Freeman, 650 F.3d 673, 680 (7th Cir. 2011);
(prosecutor's use of witness's testimony regarding codefendant's presence in drug house improper because prosecutor received letter from codefendant's attorney stating that codefendant was in prison during the time in question and thus prosecutor should have known testimony was false).

United States-V-Foster, 874 F.2d 491, 495 (8th Cir. 1988);

(prosecutor's failure to correct witness' testimony that no promises were made in exchange for testimony improper).

Morris-V-Yist, 447 F.3d 735, 744 (9th Cir. 2006);

(failure to investigate known inconsistencies in testimony to do so later supported inference that at least some of witness's testimony was false and prosecution improperly presented it).

Dow-V-Virga, 729 F.3d 1041, 1050 (9th Cir. 2003);

(prosecutor's knowing introduction of false testimony and subsequent arguments relying on that testimony improper).

Guzman-V-Sec'y of Corr., 663 F.3d 1336, 1349 (11th Cir. 2011);

(prosecutor's introduction of testimony that witness received no additional benefit from government improper because detective's knowledge of offering witness $500 reward is imputed to prosecutor).

United States-V-Iverson, 637 F.2d 799, 801-03 (D.C. Cir. 1980);

(prosecutor's failure to correct principle witness's false testimony that she had nothing to gain from testifying improper).

CHAPTER: 22

IT IS IMPROPER FOR A PROSOCUTER TO USE STAGED TESTIMONY

CASES:

Miranda-V-Bennett, 322 P.3d 171, 181 (2nd Cir. 2003);
(prosecutor's question to witness regarding evidence unknown to defense counsel improper because evidence inadmissible and concealed from defense).

United States-V-Maynard, 236 F.3d 601, 604-06 (10th Cir. 2000);
(prosecutor's question implying defendant killed man after threatening him improper because there was no other supporting evidence for allegations).

CHAPTER: 23

IT IS IMPROPER FOR A PROSECUTOR TO MISSTATE THE LAW

CASES:

United States-V-Soto-Beniquez, 356 F.3d 1, 12 (1st Cir. 2003);
(prosecutor's statement that plea of not guilty is "not a declaration of innocence" improper" because undermined presumption of innocence).

Dagley-V-Russo, 540 F.3d 8, 12 (1st Cir. 2008);
(prosecutor's argument that defendant should not be convicted of manslaughter because his action were not a "reasonable response" improper because manslaughter does not require defendant's response to be reasonable).

United States-V-Cruz, 979 F.2d 90, 93 (2nd Clr. 1986);
(prosecutor's statement that "defense has to convince you" improper but does not warrant reversal).

Chalmers-V-Mitchell, 73 F.3d 1262, 1269 (2nd Cir. 1996);
(prosecutor's reference to government's burden as "beyond a reasonable doubt, to the exclusion of a moral certainty," improper misstatement of law because it shifts burden to defendant).

Lesko-V-Lehman, 925 F.2d 1527, 1545-47 (3rd Cir. 1993);
(prosecutor's suggestion at death penalty phase that jury had duty to "even score" for two (2) murders for which defendant would be separately sentenced improper because implied jury had authority to impose death sentence for murder not before it).

United States-V-Monroe, 178 F.3d 304, 308 (5th Cir. 1999);
(prosecutor's incorrect statement of jury instruction improper misstatement).

Roe-V-Baker, 316 F.3d 557, 565-66 (6th Cir. 2002);
(prosecutor's comments that there were no mitigating factors in death sentencing case improper because false, but no prejudice because comments isolated and mitigated by curative instructions).

United States-V-Henry, 54 F.3d 367, 382-83 (6th Cir. 2008);
(prosecutor's suggestion to jurors that they would not let their children take a job with defendant improper because implied that burden of proof governed by that standard rather than reasonable doubt).

United States-V-Fenzl, 670 F.3d 778, 783 (7th Cir. 2012);
(prosecutor's statement that defendant's failure to subcontract work to a minority business constituted fraud was improper because failure was breach of contract fraud).

United States-V-Gassrope, 342 F.3d 866, 871 (8th Cir. 2003);
(prosecutor's misstatement about presumption of innocence during oral objection improper but no prejudice because remark could not have affected

verdict).

United States-V-Voice, 622 F.3d 870, 875 (8th Cir. 2010);

(prosecutor's statement of the definition of "habitually" was improper misstatement of the law).

United States-V-Sandoval-Gonzalez, 642 F.3d 717, 724-25 (9th Cir. 2011);

(prosecutor's statement that not citizens improper because burden of proof to defendant).

persons born outside U.S. are presumed incorrect statement of law that shifted)

United States-V-Perlaza, 439 F.3d 1149, 1172 (9th Cir. 2006);

(prosecutor's comment that presumption of innocence disappears when jury starts to deliberate improper).

Le-V-Mullin, 311 F.3d 1002, 1018 (10th Cir. 2002);

(prosecutor's statements discouraging jury from considering mitigating evidence offered for defendant in death penalty case improper, but no prejudice because court and defendant's attorney gave proper instructions).

Cox-V-McNeil, 638 F.3d 1356, 1361 (11th Cir. 2011);

(prosecutor's statement during closing argument that jury would have "the evidence in aggravation outweighs the evidence in mitigation, the law says you must recommend that [the defendant] die" improper misstatement of law).

United States-V-Venable, 269 F.3d 1068, 1090-91 (D.C. Cir. 2001);

(prosecutor's statement during closing argument that jury would have to disbelieve all three (3) government witness to acquit improper because false, but did not warrant relief in context of argument as a whole).

United States-V-Hall, 610 F.3d 727, 741 (D.C. Cir. 2010);

(prosecutor's statement that if it found defendant had lied "to one person one time, he can be found guilty of fraud" improper because statute required a scheme to defraud).

CHAPTER: 24

IT IS IMPROPER FOR A PROSECUTOR TO MAKE A MISSTATEMENT OF FACT

CASES:

United States-V-Ydechukwv, 11 F.3d 1101, 1105-06 (1st Cir. 1993);
(prosecutor's insinuation that defendant fabricated story about drug source improper because prosecutor knew drug source existed).

United States-V-Castro-Davis, 612 F.3d 53, 68 (1st Cir. 1993);
(prosecutor's statement confusing defendant with codefendant improper).

United States-V-Forlorma, 94 F.3d 91, 96 (2nd Cir. 1996);
(prosecutor's repeated misstatement of facts reinforcing inference defendant was aware of heroin concealed in bag improper).

United States-V-Truman, 688 F.3d 129, 144 (2nd Cir. 2012):
(prosecutor's statement that witness's cooperation agreement had been violated improper because there was no evidence government had voided the agreement).

Jackson-V-Conway, 763 F.3d 115, 143-44 (2nd Cir. 2014);
(the prosecutor in a rape case mischaracterized the evidence by asserting that, after Bonisteel "accused [Jackson] of having sex with [his] own, child," he responded, "yeah maybe, I could have").

Marshall-V-Hendricks, 307 F.3d 36, 65 (3rd Cir. 2002);
(prosecutor's mischaracterization of testimony by defense witness improper).

United States-V-Wilson, 135 F.3d 291, 297-99 (4th Cir. 1998);
(prosecutor's closing argument that defendant had committed murder improper because remarks unsupported by records, misled jury, and were prominent and well-developed).

United States-V-Murrah, 888 F.2d 24, 27 (5th Cir. 1989);
(prosecutor's reference in opening and closing arguments to witness whose testimony would implicate defendant but who was never produced improper because "inflammatory and misleading").

Hamblin-V-Mitchell, 354 F.3d 482, 495 (6th Cir. 2003);
(prosecutor's reference to repeated blows to victim improper because evidence showed victim received only one (1) blow).

United States-V-Anderson, 450 F.3d 294, 300 (7th Cir. 2006.);
(prosecutor's incorrect comment that defendants stipulated substances found were crack improper).

United States-V-Johnson, 655 F.3d 594, 601-02 (7th Cir. 2011);
(prosecutor's comment that 5 kilograms of cocaine were recovered from defendant's property improper when amount actually recovered was less than half a kilogram).

United States-V-Beckman, 222 F.3d 512, 526-27 (8th Cir. 2000);

(prosecutor's statement in closing argument that defendant charged with drug offenses lost job failed drug test improper because based on facts not in evidence).

United States-V-Kajayan, 8 F.3d 1315, 1320-22 (9th Cir. 1993);

(prosecutor's untruthful statement denying plea agreement with witness improper despite being invited by defense counsel).

United States-V-Reyes, 577 F.3d 1069, 1076-78 (9th Cir. 2009);

(prosecutor's statement that entire corporate finance department did not know of falsified report improper because prosecutor knew statement was contradicted by evidence not presented to jury).

Davis-V-Zant, 36 F.3d 1538, 1546-51 (11th Cir. 1994);

(prosecutor's closing argument that defendant fabricated last minute defense that co-defendant committed murder improper because prosecutor knew co-defendant confessed).

United States-V-Merrill, 513 F.3d 1293, 1307 (11th Cir. 2008);

(prosecutor's statement that medical examiner had seen track marks on defendant's arms improper because examiner actually testified he saw no injection site).

Lucas-V-Georgia Diagnostic and Classification, 771 F.3d 785, 804 (11th Cir. 2014);

(a prosecutor may not "misstate the facts or law in his cross-examination of witnesses" or "assum[e] prejudicial facts not in evidence").

United States-V-Watson, 171 F.3d 695, 698 (D.C. Cir. 1999);

(prosecutor's misstatement of defense witness's testimony improper because amounted to statement of facts not supported by the record/evidence).

CHAPTER: 25

IT IS IMPROPER FOR A PROSECUTOR TO COMMENT BEFORE THE JURY ON EVIDENCE THEY DO NOT INTEND ON USING

CASES:

United States -V- Lazardo, 445 F.3d 73, 86-87 (1st Cir. 2006);
(prosecutors opening argument improper because contained three statements not supported by evidence).

V.I. -V- Turner, 409 F.2d 102, 103 (3rd Circ. 1968);
(prosecutors opening statement improper because it referred to other in admissible c charges against defendant).

United States -V- Brockington, 849 F.2d 872, 875 (4th Cir. 1988);
(prosecutor's opening statement improper because it contains sufficiently questionable evidence to make it unreasonable to refer to such evidence).

United States -V- Valencia, 600 F.3d 389, 411 (5th Cir. 2010);
(prosecutor's reading of entire whistleblower letter during opening statement improper because good chance letter was impermissible hearsay).

United States -V- Steinkoetter, 593 F.2d 747, 748 (6th Cir. 1979);
(prosecutor's opening statement referring to unrelated murders improper because no evidence pertaining to the murders was later admitted).

United States -V- Dougherty, 810 F.2d 763, 767 (8th Cir. 1987);
(prosecutor's opening statement improper because it referred to witnesses prior conviction arising out of the same case).

United States -V- Thomas, 114 F.3d 228, 248 (D.C. Cir. 1997);
(prosecutors opening statement improper because prosecutor later failed to produce referenced evidence).

CHAPTER: 26

A PROSECUTOR MAY ONLY COMMENT ON
EVIDENCE THAT WAS OFFERED DURING
TRIAL WHEN HE IS MAKING HIS OPENING
OR CLOSING ARGUMENT TO THE JURY

CASES:

United States -V- Gentles, 619 F.3d 75, 82083 (1st Cir. 2010);
(prosecutor's reference to studies done on television show CSI improper because not supported by evidence).

United States -V- Salley, 651 F.3d 159, 164-65 (1st Cir. 2011);
(prosecutor's statement in closing argument that there was no suggestion that firearm was planted in defendants bedroom not improper because defense theory opened the door to prosecutors statement which properly focused on what the evidence had or had not shown).

United States -V- Forlorma, 94 F.3d 91, 94-95 (2nd Cir. 1996);
(prosecutor's statement that suits in the heroin bag fit the defendant improper because it was not supported by evidence).

United States -V- Astrangelo, 172 F.3d 288, 297-98 (3rd Cir. 1998);
(prosecutor's statement implying that defendant was the "cook" in methamphetamine conspiracy improper because it was not supported by evidence).

United States -V- Scheetz, 293 F.3d 175, 186 (4th Cir. 2002);
(prosecutor's inference from taped conversation that defendant possessed firearm improper because when tape was admitted, judge instructed jury to consider it only in relation to codefendant).

United States -V- Baptiste, 264 F.3d 578, 591-92 (5th Cir. 2010);
(prosecutor's remarks during closing improper because alleged defendants would "kill again" if not convicted).

United States -V- Rice, 607 F.3d 133, 140 (5th Cir. 2010);
(prosecutor's statement that jury could consider prior convictions for identifications purposes improper because convictions not admitted into evidence).

United States -V- Anderson, 755 F.3d 782, 796-98 (5th Cir. 2014);
(prosecutor's statement reference to coconspirator's state court conviction during rebuttal improper because unsupported by evidence admitted in trial).

DePew -V- Anderson, 311 F.3d 742, 747 (6th Cir. 2002);
(prosecutor's comment that defendant was previously involved in knife fight unrelated to indictment improper because outside of evidence offered).

Johnson -V- Mitchell, 585 F.3d 923, 938-36 (6th Cir. 2009);
(prosecutor's description of defendant as left-handed in closing argument improper because not supported by evidence at trial).

United States -V- White, 222 F.3d 363, 370-71 (7th Cir. 2000);

(prosecutor's statement in closing argument that defendant raped 13-year-old girl and sent her to hospital improper because unsupported by evidence).

United States -V- Fenzi, 670 F.3d 778, 782-83 (7th Cir. 2012);

(prosecutor's statement during closing argument that defendant committed fraud improper because not supported by record).

United States -V- Philpot, 733 F.3d 734, 745-46 (7th Cir. 2013);

(prosecutor's description of timeline of events, which suggested a coverup, improper because not supported by evidence).

United States -V- Fletcher, 322 F.3d 508, 516 (8th Cir. 2003);

(prosecutor's reference to exclude portion of witness testimony improper).

United States -V- Rodriguez, 581 F.3d 775, 803 (8th Cir. 2009);

(prosecutor statement during his closing argument asking jury to imagine victims "raw fear" improper because the government did not introduce evidence of victims fear).

United States -V- Stinson, 647 F.3d 1196, 1214 (9th Cir. 2011);

(prosecutor's questions and by hypotheticals to defense expert concerning debriefs improper debriefs not admitted into evidence).

Le -V- Mullin, 311 F.3d 1002, 1019-21 (10th Cir. 2002);

(prosecutor's reference to interactions between defendant and victim, formation of intent, misstatement of trial records, and implication that defendant had murdered before all improper because no evidence in record to support assertion).

United States -V- Lopez-Medina, 596 F.3d 716, 740 (10th Cir. 2010);

(prosecutor's statement that defendant gained weight because he stopped using methamphetamine improper because no evidence was presented of connection between cessation of methamphetamine use and weight gain).

United States -V- Tobin, 676 F.3d 1264, 1301 (11th Cir. 2012);

(prosecutor's statement that reporter wrote a "big article" in which defendant was "front and center" and that this "outed" him improper because facts were not in evidence).

United States -V- Teffera, 985 F.2d 1082, 1089 (D.C. Cir. 1993);

(prosecutor's references in argument to alleged eye contact between codefendants at time of arrest improper because not supported by evidence).

United States -V- Earle, 375 F.3d 1159, 1163-65 (D.C. Cir. 2004);

(prosecutor's inference in closing argument that defense witness lied improper because unsupported by evidence).

United States -V- Valdez, 723 F.3d 206, 208-09 (D.C. Cir. 2013);

(prosecutor's statement that coconspirator called defendant "Montana" in reference to the movie Scarface improper because unsupported by evidence).

CHAPTER: 27

IT IS IMPROPER FOR A PROSECURTOR TO USE A DEFENDANT'S POST-ARREST SILENCE AGAINST HIM IN FRONT OF THE JURY

STANDARD OF REVIEW:

Doyle -V- Ohio, 426 U.S. 610, 618-19 (1976);
(Doyle "rests on the fundamental unfairness of implicitly assuring a suspect that his silence will not be used against him and then using his silence to impeach an explanation subsequently offered at trial" which denied him a fair trial) (quoting S.D. -V- Neville, 459 U.S. 553, 565).

CASES:

United States -V- Mooney, 315 F.3d 54, 61 n.1 (1st Cir. 2002);
(prosecutor's comment on defendant's choice not to talk to police after his arrest improper).

United States -V- Nunez-Rios, 622 F.2d 1093, 1099, 1101 (2nd Cir. 1980);
(prosecutor's closing argument use of defendant's post-arrest, pre-Miranda silence to impeach defendants testimony improper).

V.I. -V- Davis, 561 F.3d 159, 167 (3rd Cir. 2009);
(prosecutor's comment on defendant's failure to provide exculpatory version of shooting improper).

Williams -V- Zahradnick, 632 F.2d 353, 355, 365 (4th Cir. 1980):
(prosecutor's use of defendant's post-arrest, post-Miranda silence to impeach defendant improper).

United States -V-Harp, 536 F.2d 601, 603 (5th Cir. 1976);
(prosecutor's referenced to defendant's post-Miranda silence to defeat their kidnapping defense improper).

Gravley -V- Mills, 87 F.3d 779, 786-88 (6th Cir. 1996);
(prosecutor's reference to defendant's post-arrest, post-Miranda silence improper).

Jaradat -V- Williams, 591 F.3d 863, 867 (6th Cir. 2010);
(prosecutor's statement emphasizing that defendant did not present explanation to police after arrest improper).

Ben-Yisayl -V- Davis, 431 F.3d 1043, 1053 (7th Cir. 2005);
(prosecutor's statement challenging defendant to explain recanted confession improper).

Fields -V- Leapley, 30 F.3d 986, 990-91 (8th Cir. 1994);
(prosecutor's use of defendant's invocation of Miranda rights improper because invocation of Miranda rights considered "silence" rather than voluntary "statements" for Miranda Purposes).

United States -V- Gentry, 555 F.3d 659, 662-63 (8th Cir. 2009);
(prosecutor's line of questions asking defendant about post-Miranda silence

improper).

Killian -V- Poole, 282 F.3d 1204, 1211 (9th Cir. 2002);

(prosecutor's repeated comments that defendant's post-arrest silence indicated she had "something to hide" improper).

Hurd -V- Terhune, 619 F.3d 1080, 1090 (9th Cir. 2010);

(prosecutor's statements inviting jury to infer guilt from post Miranda silence improper).

United States -V- Ramirez-Estrada, 749 F.3d 1129, 1134-36 (9th Cir. 2014);

(prosecutor's use of defendant's post-arrest, post-Miranda silence to impeach the defendant improper).

United States -V- Hamilton, 587 F.3d 1199, 1217 (10th Cir. 2009);

(prosecutor's elicitation of testimony regarding defendant's post-Miranda silence improper).

Hill -V- Turpin, 135 F.3d 1411, 1416-19 (11th Cir. 1998);

(prosecutor's references to defendant's post-Miranda request for counsel and assertion of right to silence improper).

CHAPTER 28:

IT IS IMPROPER FOR A PROSECUTOR TO CALL A WITNESS THAT HE KNOWS WILL INVOKE HIS FIFTH (5TH) AMENDMENT RIGHT TO SELF INCRIMINATION

STANDARD OF REVIEW:

<u>Douglas -V- Alabama</u>, 380 U.S. 415, 420 (1965);
(prosecutor's questioning of privileged codefendant resulted in reversal because lent "critical weight" to the government's case).

CASES:

<u>United States -V- ex rel Fournir</u>, 408 F.2d 539, 542 (3rd Cir. 1969);
(prosecutor's questioning of a witness in the presence of the jury when prosecutor had reason to believe that the witnesses would respond by invoking the Fifth Amendment privilege improper because it may have created an "impression or an inference unfavorable to the accused").

<u>United States -V- Brown</u>, 12 F.3d 52, 54 (5th Cir. 1994);
(prosecutor's calling defendant's husband improper because prosecutor was informed in open court and in writing of husband's intention to invoke Fifth Amendment privilege and made "conscious and flagrant effort to build a case on the unfavorable inferences which insure from a claim of the privilege").

<u>United States -V- Coppola</u>, 479 F.2d 1153, 1159-60 (10th Cir. 1973);
(prosecutors' questioning of witness who invoked his Fifth Amendment privilege 18 times was improper conduct because prosecutor knew the witness did not know the answer to the question, and the jury could draw an unfavorable inference from witness's invocation).

CHAPTER: 29

IT IS IMPROPER FOR A PROSECUTOR TO STATE BEFORE THE FJURY THE DEFENDANT'S RENTENTION OF COUNSEL INDICATES HE IS GUILTY

CASES:

Washington -V- Harris, 650 F.2d 447, 454 (2nd Cir. 1981);
(prosecutor's remark that defendant consulted counsel prior to exculpatory statement improper).

Marshall -V- Hendricks, 307 F.3d 36, 64-74 (3rd Cir. 2002);
(prosecutor's questioned two defense witnesses implying guilt from defendant's hiring attorney improper).

United States -V- Milstead, 671 F.2d 950, 953 (5th Cir. 1982);
(prosecutor's reference to defendant's retention of counsel improper).

Sizemore -V- Fletcher, 921 F.2d 667, 671 (6th Cir. 1990);
(prosecutor's intentional and repeated remarks that defendant's decision to meet with counsel immediately after incident implied guilt improper).

United States -V- Kallin, 50 F.3d 689, 692-94 (9th Cir. 1995);
(prosecutor's repeated comments on defendant's silence and retention of counsel improper).

CHAPTER: 30

MISCELLANEOUS PROSECUTOR MISCONDUCT

CASES:

United States -V- Ayala-Garcia, 574 F.3d 5, 17-18 (1st Cir. 2009);
(it was inappropriate for the prosecutor, after several inflammatory remarks, to tell the jury, "I charge you to do your job, find the defendant guilty").

Virgin Islands -V- Mills, 821 F.3d 448, 456-57 (3rd Cir. 2016);
(the prosecutor's closing violated due process when he kept saying, there's "NO" place like home. We have our house there, it's comfortable we feel safe at home. The prosecutor then began to veer off course when, instead of steering the narrative to what transpired at Clement's home, he admonished the jury to consider the safety of their home. "[Y]ou want to get home but let me tell you how home sweet home and there's NO place like home can be ruined, it can be ruined by Aswa Mills") (Must read this case).

Brown -V- Greene, 834 F.3d 506, 517-18 (3rd Cir. 2016);
(it is "error" for a prosecutor "to undo the effect of the limiting instruction" during his closing summation).

United States -V- Delgado, 631 F.3d 685, 699 (5th Cir. 2011);
(it was improper for the prosecutor to attack the defendant's credibility).

Cauthor -V- Colson, 736 F.3d 465, 476 (6th Cir. 2013);
(the prosecutor made biblical references, repeatedly referring to petitioner as "the evidence" and referring to the Lord's prayer improper. Likewise, the prosecutor's remarks amounted to a litany of the kind of remarks that courts disfavor. The prosecutor compared petitioner to two widely despised criminals of our time).

United States -V- Conney, 995 F.2d 578, 584-86 (5th Cir. 1993);
(prosecutor's questioning of two of defendant's former attorneys who invoked attorney-client privilege multiple times potentially improper, but ultimately not improper because not deliberate attempt to capitalize on failure of witnesses to testify, cautionary instruction were given, and questioning was not significant in context of lengthy testimony).

United States -V- Crumpton, 824 F.3d 519, 593 (6th Cir. 2016);
("[D]o you think that the government really wants to charge somebody that's innocent?" Was improper because it tended "to suggest that [the] defendant is guilty merely because he is being prosecuted or has been indicted").

United States -V- Resnick, 823 F.3d 888, 889 (7th Cir. 2016);
(due process violated when court allowed defendant's refusal to take polygraph test into evidence before jury).

Baldwin -V- Adams, 899 F. Supp. 2d 889, 904 (N. Dist. 2012);

(improper to state "with this kind of evidence, if you find the defendant not guilty, I mean it's almost like it's open season in East Oakland. This is what I do").

United States -V- Nobari, 574 F.3d 1065, 1077 (9th Cir. 2009);

(the testimony an argument were improper for introducing ethnic-based stereotypes that the jury could use to infer that individual defendants were guilty) (but harmless).

United States -V- Sanchez, 659 F.3d 1252, 1256 (9th Cir. 2011);

(improper statement for prosecutor to tell jury to "send a memo" urging the jury to convict "for reasons wholly irrelevant to [Sanchez's] guilt or innocence").

United States -V- Mageno, 762 F.3d 933, 949 (9th Cir. 2014);

(the government's statement that Mageno "knew she was translating for a known methamphetamine dealer" improper).

Zapata -V- Vasquez, 788 F.3d 1106, 1114-1123 (9th Cir. 2015);

([t]he prosecutor engaged in misconduct when he delivered a soliloquy in the voice of the victim, the prosecutor's comments were improper).

Wilson -V- Simmons, 536 F.3d 1064, 1118 (10th Cir. 2008);

(improper for prosecutor to call defendants "animals" and "unadulterated evil") (no plain error).

Wilson -V- Simmons, 536 F.3d 1064, 1119 (10th Cir. 2008);

(improper for prosecutor to refer to defense counsel's argument as a "smokescreen") (overwhelming evidence of guilt).

Wilson -V- Simmons, 536 F.3d 1064, 1120 (10th Cir. 2008);

(improper for prosecutor to make statement that the jury had to convict, by telling them they were "the great equalizer") (overwhelming evidence but no prejudice shown).

CHAPTER: 31

PROSECUTOR MISCONDUCT CUMULATION OF ERRORS

STANDARD OF REVIEW:

"[A] two-part test determines whether prosecutorial misconduct has occurred. See <u>Graves -V- Iowa State Pen.</u>, 614 F.3d 501, 508 (8th Cir. 2010); First, the prosecutor's conduct or remarks must have been improper, and second, the remarks or conduct must have prejudicially affected the defendant's substantial rights by depriving the defendant of a fair trial." See also United States -V- White, 241 F.3d 1015, 1023 (8th Cir. 2001). Even if one or more of the comments was improper, reversal "is appropriate only when we determine that the jury verdict reasonably could have been affected by the improper conduct." <u>United States -V- Peyro</u>, 786 F.2d 826, 831 (8th Cir. 1986).

Thus, if a petitioner, cannot show the comments or conduct deprived him of a fair trial, the court will not decide whether they were improper. Federal courts have looked to three factors to determine whether prosecutorial misconduct deprived the defendant of a fair trial. See <u>United States -V- Beeks</u>, 224 F.3d 741, 745 (8th Cir. 2000).

First, courts consider the cumulative effect of the misconduct. Second, courts examine the strength of the properly admitted evidence of the defendant's guilt. Last, courts review the curative actions taken by the District Court.

It should be noted that prosecutor misconduct as in any error raised within a writ of habeas corpus, or direct appeal, is judged and decided by the strength of evidence presented by the state supporting the defendant's guilt. The weaker the evidence of guilt against the defendant, the more likely, the prosecutor is to commit misconduct in order to secure a conviction. Keep in mind when preparing your writ, that the courts when judging prosecutorial misconduct will always look to the evidence of guilt presented at trial. This is where the harmless error analysis comes in, which will be presented herein in a later chapter.

CASES:

<u>Louisell -V- Iowa Dept. of Corr.</u>, 178 F.3d 1019, 1024 (8th Cir. 1999);

(cumulative trial errors warranted habeas relief when the prosecutors actions are improper and have "prejudicially affected the defendant's substantial rights so as to deprive the defendant of a fair trial").

<u>United States -V- Wood</u>, 207 F.3d 1222, 1237-38 (10th Cir. 2000);

(reversed conviction because of the cumulative effect of the improper denial of mid-trial acquittal on the first- and second-degree murder and evidentiary error).

<u>Cargle -V- Mullins</u>, 317 F.3d 1196 (10th Cir. 2003);

("a cumulative error analysis aggregates all error found to be harmless and analysis whether their cumulative effect on the outcome of the trial is such that collectively they can no longer be determined to be harmless") (citing United States -V- Toles, 297 F.3d 959, 972 (10th Cir. 2002).

CHAPTER: 32

OUTRAGEOUS GOVERNMENT CONDUCT

CASES:

United States -V- Therrein, 847 F.3d 9, 14 (1st Cir. 2017):

(a defendant's claim of outrageous government misconduct faces a demanding standard, permitting the dismissal of criminal charges "only in those very rare instances when the government's misconduct is so appalling and egregious as to violate due process by shocking . . . The universal sense of justice.") (quoting United States -V- Russell, 411 U.S. 423, 93 S. CT. 1637, 36 L. ED. 2d 366 (1973)).

United States -V- Twigg, 588 F.2d 373, 380-81 (3rd Cir. 1978);

(outrageous barded conviction where a government agent set up a drug lab, supplying the key ingredients to make the drugs, purchased almost all the other supplies, "was completely in charge, of the operation, and furnished all of the laboratory expertise").

CHAPTER: 33

A JURY MUST BE SELECTED FROM A FAIR CROSS SECTION OF THE COMMUNITY

The Sixth Amendment guarantees citizens of a crime the right to "a speedy and public trial, by an impartial jury . . ." The Fourteenth Amendment makes binding on the State the jury trial provisions of the Sixth Amendment, Taylor -V- Louisiana, 419 U.S. 522, 526, 95 S.Ct. 692, 41 L.ED. 2d 690 (1975). "[T]he American concept of the jury trial contemplates a jury drawn from a fair cross section of the community." Id., 419 U.S. at 527; Atwell -V-Blackburn, 800 F.2d 502 (5th Cir. 1986) (fair cross section requirement applies to grand as well as petite jury panels); Machetti -V- Linahan, 679 F.2d 236, 239 (11th Cir. 1982) (same). Selecting a jury from a representative cross section of the community "is an essential component of the Sixth Amendment right to a jury." See also Taylor -V- Louisiana, Supra, at 419 U.S. at 528. "it must be remembered that the jury is designed not only to understand the case, but also to reflect the community's sense of justice in deciding it -- as long as there are significant departures from the cross-sectional goal, biased jurors are the result -- biased in the sense that they reflect a slanted view of the community they are supposed to represent. Id., 419 U.S. at 530. "trial by jury presupposes a jury drawn from a pool broadly representative of the community as well as impartial in a specific case . . . [T]he representative of the community as well as character of the jury should be maintained, partly as assurance of a diffused impartiality and partly because sharing in the administration of justice is a phase of civic responsibility." Id., 419 U.S. at 530.

If a racial discrimination occurs in the selection process of the grand jury, the conviction must be reversed notwithstanding "overwhelming" evidence of guilt. Vasquez -V- Hillary, 474 U.S. 254, 106 S.CT. 617, 622, 88 L.ED. 2d 598 (1986). Discrimination in the selection of members of a grand jury has an effect on the fairness of the criminal trial that results from that grand jury's actions "even if a grand jury's determination of probable cause is confirmed in hindsight by a conviction in the indicted offense [since] that confirmation in no way that the discrimination did not impermissibly infect the framing of the indictment and, consequently, the nature or very existence of the proceeding to come." Id., 106 S.CT. at 623.

"When constitutional error calls into question the objectivity of those charged with bringing a defendant to judgment, a reviewing court can neither indulge a presumption of regularity nor evaluate the resulting harm." Id., 106 S.CT. at 623. "[D]iscrimination in the grand jury undermines the structural integrity of the criminal tribunal itself and is not amendable to harmless error review." Id., 106 S.CT. at 623. "Once having found discrimination in the selection of a grand jury, we simply cannot know that the need to indict would have been assessed in the same way by a grand jury properly constituted." Id., 106 S.CT. at 624. "The overriding imperative to eliminate this systemic flaw in the charging process, as well as the difficulty of assessing its effect on any given defendant, requires our continued adherence to a rule of mandatory reversal." Id., 106 S.CT. at 624.

A defendant asserting a violation of the "fair cross section" requirement need not be a member of the excluded class because "there is no rule that claims such [as these] may be made only by those defendants who are members of the group excluded from jury service." Taylor -V- Louisiana, Supra, 419 U.S. at 526, citing Peters -V- Kiff, 407 U.S. 493, 92 S.CT. 2263, 33 L.ED. 2b 83 (1972). To establish prima facie showing of a violation of this "fair cross section" requirement, a citizen must demonstrate that: (1) the group alleged to have been excluded is a distinctive group in the community; (2) the representation of the group in venires from which juries are selected is not fair and reasonable in relation to their number in the community; and (3) this under representation is the result of a systematic exclusion of the group in the jury selection process. Duren -V- Missouri, 439 U.S. 357, 99 S.CT. 664, 668, 58 L. ED. 2d 570 (1979). As for the under-representation requirement, a "defendant must demonstrate the percentage of the community made up of the group alleged to be underrepresented, for this is the conceptual benchmark for the Sixth Amendment fair cross section requirement." Id., 99 S.CT. at 688. Additionally, the defendant must show that the under representation of the group at issue "generally and on his venire, was due to their systematic exclusion in the jury selection process." Id., 99 S.CT. at 699.

Once the defendant has made prima facie showing of a systematic exclusion, the State may justify the infringement "by showing attainment of a fair cross-section to be incompatible with a significant state interest." Id., 99 S.CT. at 671. A prima facie showing of a "systematic" is made by demonstrating that the under-representation record overtime and was "inherent in the particular jury selection process utilized." Id., 99 S.CT. at 699. Intent to discriminate need not be proven since the fair cross section requirement "forbids any substantial under representation of minorities regardless of whether the state's motive is discriminatory." Aiston -V- Manson, 791 F.2d 255, 258 (2nd Cir. 1986), cert. denied, 479 U.S. 1084, 107 S.CT. 1285, 94 L.ED. 2d 143 (1987).

The cases listed above makes clear, that if a defendant is indicted by a grand jury or convicted by a petite jury that does not consist of an equal number of whites, blacks or Hispanics that does not cover a fair cross section of the community, a defendant's constitutional rights were violated, and he or she is entitled to a new trial. This is considered a structural error, which rights are fundamental and cannot be waived without the defendant signing those rights away.

CHAPTER: 34

HARMELSS ERROR VS. STRUCTURAL ERROR:
DEFINITION OF STRUCTURAL ERROR

The United States Supreme court has defined structural error, as meaning absolute rights. Absolute rights are those that cannot be waived unless the defendant waives them in open court or signs them away. Otherwise, they are never considered harmless and if they are violated, a conviction must be set aside. Below are a list of cases which support structural error. Gideon -V- Wainwright, 372 U.S. 386, 83 S.CT. 792, 9 L.ED. 2d 799 (1963) (the total deprivation of the rights to counsel at trial); Tumay -V- Ohio, 273 U.S. 510, 47 S.CT. 437, 71 L.ED. 749 (1927) (a biased judge); Vasquez -V- Hillery, 474 U.S. 254, 106 S.CT. 617, 88 L.ED. 2d 598 (1985); (unlawful exclusion of members of the defendant's race from a grand jury); McKlaskie -V- Wiggins, 4665 U.S. 168, 104 S.CT. 944, 79 L.ED.2d 122 (1984) (the denial of the right to self-representation at trial); and Waller -V- Georgia, 467 U.S. 39, 104 S.CT. 2210, 81 L.ED. 2d 81 (1984) (third denial of the right to a public trial). These errors will provide a defendant with a new trial, if violated.

DEFINITION OF HARMLESS ERROR:

An error that does not affect a party's substantial rights in the case is considered harmless error. In other words, the evidence against guilt is weighed against any error, to see if the defendant was denied a fair trial by such evidence.

Supreme Court reiterated the rarity of structural error in . . . Neder -V- United States, 572 U.S. 1, 8, 119 S.CT. 1827, 1833, 144 L.ED. 2d 35 (1999), stating that: "[I]f the defendant had counsel and was tried by an impartial and adjudicator, there is a strong presumption that any other [constitutional] errors that may have occurred are subject to harmless-error analysis. The same point about the rarity of structural error was made in Chief Justice Rehnquist's majority opinion in Fulminante.

There he listed all types of error the court had held to be subject to harmless error analysis and therefore, not structural in nature:

Clemons -V- Mississippi, 494 U.S. 738, 752-54, 110 S.CT. 1441, 1450-51, 108 L.ED. 2d 725 (1990) (unconstitutionally overbroad jury instructions at that sentencing stage of a capital case); Satterwhite -V- Texas, 436 U.S. 249, 108 S.CT. 1782, 100 L.ED 2d 284 (1988) (admission of evidence at the sentencing stage of a capital case in violation of the Sixth Amendment council claim); Carella -V- California, 491 U.S. 263, 266, 109 S.CT. 2419, 2421, 105 L.ED. 2d 218 (1983) (jury instruction containing an erroneous conclusive presumption); Pope -V- Illinois, 431 U.S. 497, 501-04, 107 S.CT. 1913, 1921-23, 95 L.ED. 2d 439 (1987) (jury instruction misstating an element of the offense); Ross -V- Clark, 478 U.S. 570 106 S.CT. 3101, 92 L.ED. 2d 460 (1988) (jury instruction containing and erroneous rebuttal presumption); Crane -V- Kentucky, 476 U.S. 683, 691, 106

S.CT. 2141, 2147, 90 L.ED. 2d 636 (1986) (erroneous exclusion of defendant's testimony regarding the circumstances of his confession); <u>Delaware -V-Vanarspall</u>, 475 U.S. 673, 106 S.CT. 1421, 89 LED. 2d 674 (1986) (restrictions on a defendant's right to cross examine a witness for bias violation of the Sixth Amendment communication clause); <u>Rushen -V- Spain</u>, 464 U.S. 114, 117-18 § n.2 104 S.CT. 454, 454-55 § n.2, 78 L.ED. 2d 267 (1983) (denial of a defendant's rights to be present at trial); <u>United States -V- Hasting</u>, 461 U.S. 499, 108 S.CT. 1974, 76 L.ED. 2d 98 (1983) (improper comment on defendant silence at trial, in violation of the Fifth Amendment self-incrimination clause); <u>Hoper -V- Evans</u>, 456 U.S. 605, 102 S.CT. 2049, 72 L.ED. 2d 367 (1982) (statute improperly forbidding trial courts giving a jury instruction on a lesser-included offense in a capital case in violation of the due process); <u>Kentucky -V- Whorton</u>, 441 U.S. 786, 99 S.CT. 2088, 60 L.ED. 2d 640 (1975) (failure to instruct the jury on the presumption of innocence); <u>Moore -V- Illinois</u>, 434 U.S. 220, 232, 98 S.CT. 458, 466, 54 L.ED. 2d 424 (1977) (admission of identification evidence in violation of the Sixth Amendment to counsel clause); <u>Brown -V- United States</u>, 411 U.S. 223, 231-32, 93 S.CT. 15665, 1570-71, 36 L.ED. 2d 208 (1973) (admission of the out-of-court statement of a non-testifying codefendant in violation of the Sixth Amendment counsel clause); <u>Milton -V- Wainwright</u>, 407 U.S. 372, 92 S.CT. 2174, 33 L.ED. 2d 1 (1972) (confession obtained in violation of <u>Massiah -V- United States</u>, 377 U.S. 201, 84 S.CT. 1199, 12 L.ED. 2d 246 (1964). <u>Chambers -V-Maroncy</u>, 399 U.S. 42, 52-53, 90 S.CT. 1975, 1981-82, 18 L.ED. 2d 419 (1970) (admission of evidence obtained in violation of the Fourth Amendment); <u>Coleman -V- Alabama</u>, 399 U.S. 1, 10-11, 90 S.CT. 1999, 2003-04, 26 L.ED. 2d 387 (1970) (denial of counsel at a preliminary hearing in violation of the Sixth Amendment confrontation clause). Basically, a petition that is denied due to harmless-error or no prejudiced shown means that the evidence of guilt was more powerful, overwhelming, or convincing, in the court's eyes.

CHAPTER: 35

THE EIGHTH AMENDMENT AND JUVENILE OFFENDERS

The Eighth Amendment to the United States Constitution forbids the imposition of cruel and unusual punishment. "Cruel and unusual" has not been interpreted to be synonymous with the term "unfair." Instead, the jurisprudence of the United States Supreme Court has interpreted the Eighth Amendment to categorically exclude certain punishments for certain classes of offenders. In 2005, the Supreme Court ruled that juveniles cannot be sentence to death. See <u>Roper -V- Simmons</u>, 543 U.S. 551, 125 S. CT. 1133 (2005). In 2010, the court followed by holding that juveniles could not be sentence to life without parole for non-homicide crimes. See <u>Graham -V- Florida</u>, 560 U.S. 48, 130 S.CT. 2011 (2010). Then in 2012, the court held that those who were juveniles at the time a homicide was committed may not be sentence to mandatory life sentence without the possibility of parole. See <u>Miller -V- Alabama</u>, 132 S. CT. 2455 (2012). Finally in 2016, the United States Supreme Court decided <u>Montgomery -V- Louisiana</u>, 135 S.CT. 1546 (2016) (holding that Miller applies retroactively under Teague.

CHAPTER: 36

ACTUAL INNOCENCE CLAIMS AND FEDERAL COURTS

As noted in several previous sections, federal courts are only slightly more relaxed when considering claims involving actual innocence (meaning that the petitioner is innocent-in-fact, not simply that the state cannot meet its burden of proof.) A habeas corpus petitioner may overcome many of the above procedural barriers if he or she can show that it is "more likely than not that no reasonable juror would have convicted the [petitioner]." See McQuiggin -V- Perkins, 133 S.CT. 1924, 1931 (2015) (citing Schlup -V- Delo, 513 U.S. 293, 115 S.CT. 851 (1995)). Well federal courts are to be more forgiving of the procedural errors of a petitioner who makes a satisfactory showing of innocence, unnecessary delay in bringing a habeas corpus petition bears on whether we leave will be granted. Id. at 1986. However, in Herrerra -V- Collins, 506 U.S. 390, 417 (1993). The court in Herrerra left open the possibility that in a capital case, "a truly persuasive demonstration of 'actual innocence' made after trial would render the execution of a defendant unconstitutional if there was no state avenue of post-conviction relief, even if conviction was the product of a fair trial, thereby warranting federal habeas relief. Id. At 417. Nonetheless, such relief would be rare, as the "threshold showing for such an assumed right would necessarily be extraordinarily high." Id. At 417. House -V- Bell, 547 U.S. 518, 665 (2006) (Same). The court stated in Lopez -V- Miller, 915 F.Supp.2d 373, 382 (Eastern Dist. New York 2013), the court so stated, "To establish a "gateway" claim of actual innocence and thus overcome his procedural default, Lopez must demonstrate using '"new reliable evidence"' that it is "more likely than not . . . [that] no reasonable juror would find him guilty beyond a reasonable doubt or to remove the double negative, that more likely than not any reasonable juror would have reasonable doubt." Id. At 541 (quoting House -V- Bell, 547 U.S. 518, 126 S.CT. 2064, 165 L.ED. 2d 1 (2006), and Schlup -V- Delo, 513 U.S. 298, 324, 125 S.CT. 851, 130 S.ED. 2d 308 (1996)). Based on the weakness of the prosecution's case and the new evidence Lopez has presented since trial, the court concludes that any reasonable juror would have reasonable doubt as to guilt."

As can be seen by federal court precedent, it is not impossible to prevail on a claim of actual innocence, especially, when there is a constitutional violation. See Rivas -V- Fischer, 780 F.3d 529, 550-52 (2nd Cir. 2015) (habeas relief granted because petitioner produced credible and compelling evidence which called into serious doubt evidence linking petitioner to crime and counsel's deficient performance prejudiced defendant).

However, when the petitioner predicates his claim of actual innocence on an asserted constitutional error at trial to avoid a state procedural bar, the miscarriage of justice inquiry is governed by the standard of Murray -V- Carrier, 477 U.S. 478

(1986). Case law supports the contention that a claim of actual innocence is not dead in federal court.

CHAPTER: 37

28 U.S.C. § 2254 HABEAS CORPUS RELIEF FOR STATE PRISONERS

This book's main goal is to assist pro se litigants and attorneys find and locate favorable case law with respect to prosecutorial misconduct, as well as assisting them in putting together a proper writ to be filed in the Federal District Court to challenge their state or federal convictions under the Anti-Terrorism and Effective Death Penalty Act (AEDPA). Under the AEDPA a habeas petitioner only gets one bite at the apple. Therefore, this book will guide you step by step in preparing your writ to make sure you follow all procedures in crime lines, so there is no default.

A. <u>DISTRICT COURT PETITION PROCEDURE</u>:

Once a habeas petitioner has carefully and accurately completed the necessary forms for filing a petition, the petitioner should follow the forms instructions for filing. A petitioner may choose to file the petition either in the District Court presiding over the county in which they were convicted or the District Court presiding over the county in which they are presently incarcerated.

The incarcerating county may transfer it back to the District Court in the region where the petitioner was convicted, or petitioner may request the incarcerating county's District Court to maintain the action there. The process in the District Court typically unfolds as follows, once a petition is filed:

1. Petitions are usually reviewed by magistrate judges, and less often are reviewed directly by District Court judges. If, after initial review the court decides further discussion of the merits of a petition, they will issue an order to show cause to the Attorney General's office of that state.

2. The Attorney General's office, upon the show cause order will reply to the merits of the petition, serving both the petitioner and the court with their response.

3. A petitioner may, but is not required to, file a response to the State's answer. However, the court may compel a petitioner to do so.

4. In rare instances, as discussed more extensively further on a federal court will order an evidentiary hearing on the merits of the petitioners claim. If an evidentiary hearing is ordered, the petitioner will be brought to the court by way of a writ of habeas corpus ad testificandem. The amount of time for this hearing to be ordered may vary depending on the District Court in which the application is filed.

5. Magistrate judges, after considering the merits of a petitioners claim will make a recommendation to the more authoritative District Court judges, entering a "Report and Recommendation" or Findings, conclusions, and Recommendations. After the magistrate judge's filing a petitioner has ten days to file written objections to the courts recommendations, or longer if authorized by the court.

Failure to file written objections waves most matters except for those constituting "clear error," a high standard of proof. The same applies to objecting to some issues and not others. Those issues not objected to are deemed to be waived unless clear error has occurred.

6. A District Court judge will review the magistrate judge's report to determine whether relief should be granted or denied. The District Court judge may adopt the magistrate judge's findings, but the District Court is not bound by them.

See Braden -V- 30th Jud. Cir. Of Ky., 410 U.S. 484, 497 (1973) (habeas petition proper when filed in district where petitioner convicted or confined); Story -V- Collins, 920 F.2d 1247, 1251 (5th Cir. 1991) (habeas petition proper when filed in district where petitioner convicted or confined); Gall -V- Scroggy, 603 F.3d (2010) (same); Walker -V- Lockhart, 620 F.2d 683, 684 n.1 (8th Cir. 1990) (same); Pischke -V- Litscher, 178 F.3d 497, 499 (7th Cir. 1999) (same); Eagle -V- Lenahan, 279 F.3d 926, 933 n.9 (11th Cir. 2001) (same).

B. FEDERAL HABEAS CORPUS REVIEW:

whereas common state habeas corpus proceedings can be relatively straight forward, federal habeas corpus petitions often fail due to settle, yet complex procedural errors. The district court's most common reasons for declining a petition for writ of habeas corpus include (1) broad waiver of claims due to the entry of a plea; (2) the petitioner not being in custody; (3) untimely filing; (4) the petition having been filed successively; (5) the claims not being fully exhausted in state court; (6) the claim being procedurally defaulted; (7) the state court having not engaged in an unreasonable application of clearly established federal law; (8) the claim depending on facts which are not attainable in a federal evidentiary hearing, and (9) the claim not being "cognizable" on habeas corpus review. As any procedural error tends to prevent a habeas corpus petition from being heard on its merits in federal court, it is unsurprisingly rare for a federal court to reach the merits of a petitioner's claim.

C. RESTRAINED IN YOUR LIBERTY:

In order to apply for a writ of habeas corpus, a habeas applicant must either be incarcerated or some other sort of restraint on his or her liberty. See 28 U.S.C. § 2241 (c)(3);; Spencer -V- Kemna, 523 U.S. 1, 7 (1998) ("in custody" requirement satisfied as long as petitioner is incarcerated when petition filed); Leitao -V- Reno, 311 F.3d 453, 455 (1st Cir. 2002) (same); Perez -V- Greiner, 296 F.3d 123, 125 (2nd Cir. 2002) (same); Smith -V- Ashcroft, 295 F.3d 425, 427 (4th Cir. 2002) (same); Zalawadia -V- Ashcroft, 371 F.3d 292, 296 (5th Cir. 2004) (same); Lopez -V- Weinaur, 332 F.3d 507, 510 (8th Cir. 2003) (same); Zegarra -V- Gomez, 314 F.3d

1124, 1127 (9th Cir. 2003) (same); Mays -V- Dinwiddie, 580 F.3d 1136, 1139 (10th Cir. 2009) (same).

In short, a petitioner must be in "Custody." In Carafas -V- Lavallee, 391 U.S. 234, 88 S.CT. 1556 (1968), The United States per Supreme Court held that the petitioners case was not moot (that he was no longer in "custody") when he was unconditionally released from prison while his petition was still pending.

However, the above rule does not require that petitioner be in actual, physical custody, however, see Rumsfield -V- Padilla, 582 U.S. 426, 124 S.CT. 2711 (2004), parole release may constitute custody for purposes of habeas corpus. See Jones -V- Cunninghamm, 371 U.S. 236, 53 S.CT. 373 (1968); Wottlin -V- Flemming, 136 F.3d 1032 (5th Cir. 1998) (same). Therefore, it is clear that a petitioner must be in some sort of restraint whenever it be supervised release, probation, or parole.

D.   DETERMINING WHAT COGNIZABLE CLAIMS TO RAISE:

The determination of whether a claim is cognizable in heaviest proceedings is a determination of whether it is the type of claim most appropriate for habeas corpus proceedings. The category of cognizable federal claims is fairly expansive, encompassing most constitutional violations. It is well settled law that most if not all prosecutorial misconduct claims violate the due process clause of the Fourteenth Amendment to the United States Constitution. For example, see below:

1.   Did the prosecutor use an informant as an agent of the state to obtain an illegal statement/confession?

If the prosecutor used an informant or another inmate to obtain a confession outside the presence of the defendant's lawyer, in violates due process, as well as the right to a fair trial. See Chapter 2 of this book.

2.   Did the prosecutor express his personal opinion about the guilt of the defendant?

If a prosecutor in opening or closing summation to the jury or even during trial expressed that he thought the defendant was guilty it violates due process. See Chapter 3 of this book.

3.   Did the prosecutor make remarks about the defendant?

If the prosecutor made any remarks about the defendant during his summation to the jury, or during trial it violates due process. See Chapter 4 of this book.

4.   Does prosecutor make improper remarks about defense counsel?

If the prosecutor made improper comments about defense counsel during his opening or closing summation to the jury, or during the trial, it violates due process. See Chapter 5 of this book.

5.   Did the prosecutor make improper comments about defense witnesses?

If the prosecutor makes improper comments about defense witnesses it violates due process. See chapter 6 of this book.

6. Did the prosecutor make improper comments about a defense witnesses credibility?

If the prosecutor asked a witness to comment on the credibility of another witness it violates due process. See Chapter 7 of this book.

7. Did the prosecutor act as an expert on a subject?

If the prosecutor explained the situation to the jury as though an expert would, it violates due process. See Chapter 8 of this book.

8. Did the prosecutor point out to the jury that the defendant did not testify?

If the prosecutor expressed his opinion about the defendant's failure to testify, he is violating due process. See Chapter 9 of this book.

9. Did the prosecutor comment on the defendants prior convictions or any guilty pleas?

Did the prosecutor in your case tell the jury that you had a prior conviction or how pled guilty before? If so, it violates due process. See Chapter 10 of this book.

10. Did the prosecutor make comments concerning the prior bad acts on the defendants codefendants?

If the prosecutor explained to the jury that the defendant's codefendants had prior convictions or unadjudicated offense, it violates due process. See Chapter 11 of this book.

11. Did the prosecutor make any comments while questioning the defendant coconspirators about any bad acts regarding the defendant?

If the prosecutor made any improper comments about the defendant's coconspirators on any bad acts regarding the defendant, it violates due process. See chapter 12 of this book.

12. Did the prosecutor vouch for credibility of his witnesses?

If the prosecutor vouched for the credibility of his own witnesses at trial, it violates due process. See Chapter 13 of this book.

13. Did the prosecutor prosecute for vindictive reasons?

If the prosecutor prosecuted the defendant for vindictive reasons, it violates due process. See Chapter 14 of this book.

14. Did the prosecutor withhold exculpatory evidence?

If the prosecutor withheld exculpatory evidence in violation of the Brady Doctrine, it violates due process. See Chapter 15 of this book.

15. Did the prosecutor destroy exculpatory evidence in your case?

If the prosecutor destroyed potentially exculpatory evidence in bad faith violated due process. See Chapter 16 of this book.

16. <u>Did the prosecutor breach a plea agreement in your case?</u>

If the prosecutor breached his own plea agreement in your case. And violates due process. See Chapter 17 of this book.

17. <u>Did the prosecutor in your case use his own office to support his credibility to prosecute the case?</u>

If the prosecutor used his own credibility to prosecute you at trial, your due process rights were violated. See Chapter 18 of this book.

18. <u>Did the prosecutor testify as a witness at your trial?</u>

If the prosecutor testified as a witness at your trial, your right to due process was violated. See Chapter 19 of this book.

19. <u>Did the prosecutor in his opening or closing summation asked the jury to act as a conscience for the community?</u>

If the prosecutor asked the jury to act as a conscience of the community, it violated your right to due process. See Chapter 20 of this book.

20. <u>Did the prosecutor allow witness to testify falsely in your case?</u>

If the prosecutor allowed a witness to testify falsely without correcting the testimony, you right to due process was violated. See Chapter 21 of this book.

21. <u>Did the prosecutor in your case use staged testimony?</u>

If the prosecutor used staged testimony to obtain a conviction in your case, your right to due process was violated. See Chapter 22 of this book.

22. <u>Did the prosecutor misstate the law in your case?</u>

If the prosecutor in your case misstated the law to the jury, it was a violation of due process. See Chapter 23 of this book.

23. <u>Did the prosecutor in your case make a misstatement of the law?</u>

If the prosecutor made a misstatement of the facts in your case, it violated due process. See chapter 24 of this book.

24. <u>Did the prosecutor make comments about evidence that they do not intend on using?</u>

If the prosecutor made comments about evidence it does not intend to use, it violates due process. See Chapter 25 of this book.

25. <u>A prosecutor may only comment on evidence he is going to use at trial when he is making his opening and closing arguments.</u>

When making his opening and closing summation if the prosecutor goes outside the evidence he is going to use at trial, it violates due process. See Chapter 26 of this book.

26. <u>Did the prosecutor make comments on the defendant's post arrest silence?</u>

If the prosecutor made improper comments on the defendants post arrest silence it violates his right to due process. See Chapter 27 of this book.

27. <u>Did the prosecutor calling witness that he knew would invoke his Fifth Amendment right?</u>

If the prosecutor called a witness that he knew would invoke his Fifth Amendment rights, it violated due process. See Chapter 28 of this book.

28. <u>Did the prosecutor state before the jury that the defendant's retention of counsel indicated guilt?</u>

If the prosecutor comments that because the defendant retained an attorney he is guilty, violates due process. See Chapter 29 of this book.

29. <u>Did the prosecutor commit outrageous conduct?</u>

If the prosecutor or agents committed outrageous conduct to obtain a conviction, it violates due process among other rights. See Chapter 32 of this book.

30. <u>Was the jury or grand jury in your case selected from a fair cross section of the community?</u>

If the jury or grand jury in your case was not selected from a fair cross section of the community your right to due process was violated. See Chapter 33 of this book.

31. <u>Were you a juvenile at the time you were sentence to a life sentence in prison with or without parole?</u>

If you were sentence to life with or without parole your Eighth Amendment rights were violated. See Chapter 35 of this book.

After determining what claims you can raise in your federal writ it is then time to decide whether your it is timely as a matter of the AEDPA.

E. <u>A 2254 PETITION MUST BE FILED WITHIN ONE YEAR OF</u>:

1. The final judgement imposing sentence;

2. The denial of your appeal by an intermediate appellate court, the state's highest court, or the Supreme Court, whichever date is later; or

3. Under the United States Supreme Court's decision in <u>Jimenez -V- Quarterman</u>, 555 U.S. 113, 129 S.CT. 681 (2009), a conviction is not "final" under the terms of its original mandate under 28 U.S.C. § 2254(d)91)(A) if the court grants an out-of-time appeal.

F. <u>EXHAUSTION REQUIREMENTS</u>:

A petitioner must exhaust his or her state court remedies before federal habeas corpus review can occur. If the state courts have been given their fullest opportunities to hear the claim, then the federal district courts within the states may hear a habeas corpus petition.

However, exhaustion is not required if there is an absence of available State corrective process or certain circumstances render such process ineffective to protect the [petitioner's] rights. See 28 U.S.C. § 2254(c); and § 2254(b)(1). <u>Justice</u>

of Bos. Court -V- Lydon, 466 U.S. 294, 302-03 (1984) (exhaustion requirement satisfied by presentation of claim on appeal to the State Supreme Court from denial of motion to dismiss); See also Rolan -V- Coleman, 680 F.3d 311, 319, 325-26 (3rd Cir. 2012) (exhaustion requirement satisfied because no procedural default and prosecutorial misconduct claims sufficiently identified); Carty -V- Thaler, 583 F.3d 244, 257 (5th Cir. 2009).

Moreover, if a petitioner presents a District Court with a mix of exhausted and unexhausted claims, the court will usually decline to hear the case, unless the petitioner shows good cause for his or her failure to exhaust available state remedies. In that event, the District Court will "stay in abate" the exhausted claims while the unexhausted claims proceed in state court. See Rhines -V- Weber, 544 U.S. 269, 125 S.CT. 1528 (2005). Nonetheless, a petitioner that submits such a mixed petition may either (1) return to the state courts to litigate the unexhausted claims so they can be presented together in a single petition or (2) amend the habeas petition to present only exhausted claims to the federal District Court. See Rose -V- Lundy, 455 U.S 509, 510 (1982) (plurality opinion), abrogated in party by Rhines 544 U.S. at 269, however when a petitioner adds an unexhausted claim after the federal court reaches its decision, the circuit courts, rather than dismissing the petition, may rule on the exhausted claims and refuse to rule on the unexhausted claims. See Chandler -V- Jones, 813 F.2d 773, 777 n.4 (6th Cir. 1987). This makes clear, to be sure, that each and every claim you intend to raise in your federal habeas corpus, has been properly presented to the state's highest court.

CHAPTER: 38

HABEAS CORPUS-AEDPA: STANDARD FOR GRANTING 2244 WRIT

State federal habeas corpus 28 U.S.C. § 2254(d)(1)(2) and (e)(1) shall not be granted unless:

(d) an application for writ of habeas corpus on behalf of a person in custody pursuant to the judgment of a state court should not be granted with respect to any claim that was educated on the merits unless:

(1) resulted in a decision that was contrary to or involved an unreasonable application of, clearly established federal law, as determined by the Supreme Court of the United States, or

(2) resulted in a decision that was an unreasonable determination of the facts in light of the evidence presented in the State Court proceeding.

(e)(1) in a proceeding pursuant to the judgment of a State Court, a determination of a factual issue made by a State Court shall be presumed to be correct. The applicant shall have the burden of rebutting the presumption by clear unconvincing evidence.

1. 28 U.S.C. § 2254(d)(1) "Contrary to" definition:

The contrary to clause of § 2254(d)(1), means the state applied a rule different from the governing law as set forth in Supreme Court cases, or if it decides a case differently than the Supreme Court has done on a set of materially indistinguishable facts. For example, see Nappi -V- Yelich, 793 F.3d 246, 250-51 (2nd Cir. 2015) (state court denial of opportunity for a defendant to cross examine main witness regarding motive was contrary to clearly established federal law); Tassin -V- Cain, 517 F.3d 770, 779-80 (5th Cir. 2008) (state court failure to disclose witness's expectation of leniency in sentencing contrary to federal law).

2. 28 U.S.C. § 2254(d)(1) "Unreasonable Application" definition:

Be unreasonable Application clause of § 2254(d) (1), means that a state court identifies correct legal rule but unreasonably applies it to the facts of the case, or (2) unreasonably extends the legal principle to new context to which it should not apply or unreasonably refuses to extend the principle to new context. See William -V- Taylor, 529 U.S. 405 (2000). The application must be objectively unreasonable, not merely incorrect. See Bell -V- Cone, 535 U.S. 685, 694 (2002); See also Parker -V- Matthews, 12 S.CT. 2148, 2153 (2012). A great case on point with book is, Lewis -V- Conn. – Comm'r of Corr., 790 F.3d 109, 121-22 (2nd Cir. 2015) (state court unreasonable because imposing affirmative due diligence requirement on defendant to discover exculpatory information violated Brady).

3. "Clearly Established" Federal Law Definition:

Clearly established federal law to be used in an analysis under §2254(d)(1) is the law at the time of the last state court adjudication on the merits. See Greene -V- Fisher, 132 S.CT. 38, 44-45 (2011); See also Lockyer -V- Andrarde, 538 U.S. 63,

71 (2003) (clearly established refers to holdings, as opposed to dicta, of Supreme Court decisions at the time of the state court decision).

4. <u>28 U.S.C. § 2254(d)(2) "Unreasonable Determination of the facts" definition</u>:

An unreasonable determination of the facts does not pass muster, to warrant habeas corpus relief under 2254(d)(2); rather habeas relief may be afforded to a state prisoner only if his confinement also violates federal law. See <u>Wilson -V- Corcoran</u>, 562 U.S. 1, 5-6 (2010); See also <u>Rice -V- Collins</u>, 546 U.S. 333, 338-39 (2006) (state court acceptance of prosecution's race neutral explanation for striking African American juror not unreasonable determination of facts); See <u>Pruitt -V- Neal</u>, 788 F.3d 248, 267 (7th Cir. 2015) (state court determination that defendant was not intellectually disabled was unreasonable determination of facts because reliable test scores consistently indicated sub average intellectual functioning). This part shows that evidence is needed to support the red not merely the defendant's conclusory allegations.

5. <u>28 U.S.C. § 2254(e)(1) Definition</u>:

This part of the AEDPA is extremely difficult. The standard as mentioned, is "by clear and convincing evidence." This is the second hardest standard in law, just below Beyond a reasonable doubt. In this instance, a state court, may grant relief only, if the petitioner shows evidence that is clear and convincing. See 28 U.S.C. § 2254(e)(1); see also <u>Miller-El -V- Cockrell</u>, 537 U.S. 322, 341 (2003) (presumption of correctness overcome because district court "accepted without question the state court's evaluation of the demeanor of the prosecutors and jurors trial). The three standards as shown above are demanding, but not difficult to overcome. An easy way to explain this standard is the AEDPA, forbids, review of claims which the state court denied on the merits of the claim, so long as (1) the state court did not render a decision contrary to or involving an unreasonable application of clearly establish federal law or (2) make an unreasonable determination of the facts in light of the evidence presented before it. This provision allows for substantial breathing room for the state court decision making, even providing room for the state to render decision with which many jurists would strongly debate. Perhaps counterintuitively, this rule applies even where a state court renders a decision without a written opinion. See <u>Harrington -V- Richter</u>, 562 U.S. 86, 131 S.CT. 770 (2011). His state court legal analysis will only be overturned under this rule if all reasonable jurists would disagree with the state courts analysis. See <u>Williams -V- Taylor</u>, 529 U.S. 362, 120 S.CT. 1495 (2000). It courts determination of the facts is presumed to be controlling, but a petitioner may rebut that presumption by clear and convincing evidence. See <u>Nelson -V- Quarterman</u>, 472 F.3d 287 (5th Cir. 2006).

H. PROCEDURAL DEFAULT:

This reason for rejecting a habeas petitioner is particularly common:

Procedural default occurs where the petitioner forfeited his right to pursue the claim in compliance with state procedural rules. Coleman -V- Thompson, 501 U.S. 722, 111 S.CT. 2546 (1991). His case predating AEDPA, but which still holds merit, the Supreme Court held that where a state court denies a habeas application for procedural reasons, and that procedural reason is an "independent and adequate" state ground for denying the claim, that claim will not be considered federally, either. As with the contemporaneous objection rule, as shown in state courts, failure to make a contemporaneous objection in state court may cause federal procedural default. See Wainwright -V- Sykes, 433 U.S. 72, 97 S.CT. 2497 (1977); but see Miller -V- Estelle, 677 F.2d 1080 (5th Cir. 1982) (holding that where the state court did not rely on failure to contemporaneously object did not cause procedural default).

Likewise, other procedural rules may bar federal review. See for example Ramirez -V- Estelle, 678 F.2d 604 (5th Cir. 1982) (as the defense failed to move for a continuance when it was discovered that the state had withheld Brady evidence, the claimed barred from federal review). To overcome procedural default, the petitioner must show either both (1) cause and (2) prejudice, or (3) that a fundamental miscarriage of justice will occur if the petition is not heard. Cause must be derived from sources which cannot be attributed to the petitioner. See Murray -V- Carrier, 477 U.S. 478, 106 S.CT. 2639 (1986).

as attorneys are seen as working in concert with their clients, attorney error is generally not enough to satisfy cause, although complete abandonment in state court by a petitioner's attorney may suffice. See Maples -V- Thomas, 132 S.CT. 912, 924 (2012). To prove prejudice, a petitioner must prove that his or her claim was meritorious. See Wainwright -V- Sykes, 433 U.S. 72, 97 S.CT. 2497 (1977) (suggesting that prejudice reexamined by the damage done by the admission of the petitioners confession).

Of course, in order for a state procedural matter to bar federal review, the petitioner must have been given an "adequate" chance to address his or her claim in state court. For example, in some states which allow claims of ineffective assistance of counsel to be raised on direct appeal, failure to raise it on direct appeal may not be an adequate ground to deny federal relief, as it is virtually impossible to review trials counsel's effectiveness on direct appeal. Trevino -V- Thaler, 133 S.CT. 1911 (2013); see also Martinez -V- Ryan, 132 S.CT. 1309 (2012).

Here are some cases that overcome procedural default. Jackson -V- Amaral, 729 F.2d 41, 44 (1st Cir. 1984) (federal habeas review not precluded by failure to raise voir dire objection under direct appeal, as required by state procedural law, because state court disregarded procedural default and ruled on merits of federal claim); <u>Brown -V- Greiner</u>, 409 F.3d 523, 532 (2nd Cir. 2005) (federal habeas review not precluded because state court ruled on merits of Apprendi claim); <u>Villot -V- Varner</u>, 373 F.3d 327, 336 (3rd Cir. 2004) (federal habeas review not precluded because state trial court did not mention procedural basis for ruling and state Supreme Court decision presumed to rest on same grounds).

The above shown cases are an example of how a habeas corpus petitioner may start his research in overcoming a procedural default. Therefore, while the procedural default doctrine is demanding, it is not impossible to overcome.

I. <u>EQUITABLE-TOLLING</u>:

Under the AEDPA, a habeas petitioner must file within a one-year statute of limitations, in order for their petition to be considered on the merits. There is an exception which can be forced in § 2244(d)(1)(A). See <u>Green -V- Fisher</u>, 132 S.CT. 38 (2011) ("finality occurs when direct state appeals have been exhausted in a petition for writ of certiorari from this court has become time barred or has been disposed of). Once a petitioner properly files an application for writ of habeas corpus in the state District Court, in which they are convicted, the one-year time period is frozen, or "tolled." See <u>Lawrence -V- Florida</u>, 549 U.S. 327, 127 S.CT. 1079 (2007). Improperly filed petitions do not toll the limitation period. See <u>Wardlaw -V- Cain</u>, 541 F.3d 275 (5th Cir. 2008). Courts construe the AEDPA limitation period strictly and will only consider late petitions if the petitioner has (1) pursued his or her rights diligently, and (2) some extraordinary circumstances stood in his or her way. <u>Lawrence -V- Florida</u>, 549 U.S. at 107 (2007).

It is generally not enough that either the petitioner or his attorney miscalculated the time limit for filing. That is because petitioners are not entitled to effective assistance in habeas corpus proceedings. Mere attorney negligence is not enough to justify review of a petitioners writ outside of the statute of limitations. See <u>Holland -V- Florida</u>, 560 U.S. 631, 130 S.CT. 2549 (2010). While the AEDPA deadline is not absolute barrier to claims of actual innocence, federal courts will nevertheless, consider the length of, and reasons for a delay in considering whether to appeal a petition for writ of habeas corpus which alleges actual innocence. See <u>McQuire -V- Perkins</u>, 133 S.CT. 1924 (2013).

Next, a federal court may consider whether to hold a live evidentiary hearing. See below to learn about evidentiary hearings.

J. <u>EVIDENTIARY HEARINGS</u>:

If a petitioner fails to adequately develop the facts of his or her case in state court, then generally speaking, he or she will not be allowed an evidentiary hearing under § 2254(e)(2). Only if the claim (1) relies on a new rule of constitutional law which applies retroactively, and that new rule was not available when the petitioner was in state court, or (2) the facts which need to be developed could not have been previously discovered through the exercise of due diligence with the federal courts consider granting an evidentiary hearing. Carter -V- Duncan, 819 F.3d 931, 950-51 n. 24 (7th Cir. 2016) ("diligence will require in the usual case that the prisoner, at a minimum, seek an evidentiary hearing in state court in the manner prescribed state law"). (emphasis added) (We, therefore, do not believe that § 2254(e)(2) stands as a bar to our consideration of his request for a hearing in federal court). See also Runningeagle -V- Ryan, 825 F.3d 970, 990 (9th Cir. 2016) (we review for an abuse of discretion in district court's determination that petitioner is not entitled to an evidentiary hearing) (citing Hurles -V- Ryan, 752 F.3d 768, 777 (9th Cir.)(cet. Denied, 135 S.CT. 710, 190 L.ED. 2d 461 (2014). Likewise, see Fulton -V- Graham, 802 F.3d 257, 266 (2nd Cir. 2015) (it is our view that a habeas petitioner generally demonstrates that requisite diligence when, as here, he requests an evidentiary hearing in conjunction with a § 440.10 motion that concerns out of court conduct) (citing Drake -V- Portuondo, 321 F.3d 338, 346-47 (2nd Cir. 2003).

As mentioned, if one of the two exceptions above is shown, the petitioner must also show by clear and convincing evidence that no reasonable factfinder would have found the petitioner guilty but for the constitutional violation. However, following the supreme court's decision in Cullen -V- Pinholster, 131 S.CT. 1388 (2011), it is extraordinarily difficult to obtain a federal evidentiary hearing. The United States Supreme Court's holding in Pinholster, Supra, significantly restricts federal courts from holding evidentiary hearings. Under Pinholster, Supra federal courts may not consider new evidence in reviewing whether the state court's decision was contrary to or unreasonably applied clearly established federal law under § 2254(d)(1). See Pinholster, 131 S.CT. at 1400; see also Pape -V- Thaler, 645 F.3d 281, (5th Cir. 2011). The consequence is that in most cases come up federal courts will not allow new evidence to be discovered, no matter how substantial when reviewing a state court's decision which was made on the merits and did not involve an unreasonably termination of the facts. While § 2254(e)(2) is very demanding, it is not impossible.

K. FILING A CERTIFICATE OF APPEALIBILITY (COA):

Before a petitioner can appeal to the Court of Appeals, the appeals court must grant him a COA. 28 U.S.C. § 2253(c)(1)(A). Courts may grant a COA only if the petitioner makes a "substantial showing of the denial of a constitutional right." Id. § 2253(c)(2). See Milton -V- Miller, 812 F.3d 1252, 1263 (10th Cir. 2016). This requires a "showing that reasonable jurists could debate whether (or, for that matter, agree that) the petition should have been resolved in a different manner or that the issues presented were adequate to deserve encouragement to proceed further." <u>Slack -V- McDaniels</u>, 529 U.S. 473, 484, 120 S.CT. 1595, 146 L.ED.2d 542 (2000) (quotation marks omitted). To obtain a COA after District Court has rejected a petitioner's constitutional claims on the merits, the petitioner must demonstrate that reasonable jurists would find the district court's assessment of the [petitioners constitutional claims debatable or wrong to obtain a COA. Id].

It should be noted, if the state loses in federal court, they are allowed to appeal directly to the Court of Appeals, instead of requesting a COA.

L. <u>SUCCESSIVE PETITIONS</u>:

Under 28 U.S.C. § 2244(b)(1), a claim presented in a second or successive habeas petitions "shall be dismissed" without consideration of its merits. Under 2244(b)(2), a claim brought in a second or successive habeas petition which was not included in the first will likewise, be dismissed, unless it falls under one of two exceptions. Under the second exception, a claim first raised in a second or successive petition is not barred if (i) the facts underlying the claim could not have previously been discovered with due diligence, and (ii) facts of the claim shows by clear and convincing evidence, but further constitutional error, no reasonable fact Finder would have found the petitioner guilty of the offense. Below are cases that support a successive petition. <u>Quezada -V- Smith</u>, 624 F.3d 514, 521-22 (2nd Cir. 2010) (petitioner made prima facie case of witness perjury and Brady violation and therefore could continue with successive habeas petition); <u>Cooper -V- Woodford</u>, 358 F.3d 1117, 1123 (9th Cir. 2004) (petitioner made prima facie case of Brady violation with sworn declaration that controverted evidence presented at trial and therefore could continue with successive habeas petition).

However, before filing a second or successive petition for a habeas corpus, a petitioner must request permission from a three-judge panel of the Circuit Court of appeals. 28 U.S.C. 2244(b)(3); See also <u>Ochoa -V- Workmen</u>, 669 F.3d 1130, 1140-41 (10th Cir. 2012) (District Court had jurisdiction over successive petition because petitioner first saw it and was given authorization of the circuit).

Basically, unless a Court of Appeals allow a second or successive petition to be filed, a District Court does not make jurisdiction to entertain.

M. <u>APPOINTMENT OF COUNSEL</u>:

It makes no sense, but a heaviest petitioner, has no right to appointment of counsel, in federal habeas corpus proceedings, except any capital case. See <u>Pennsylvania -V- Finley</u>, 481 U.S. 551, 555-56, 96 L.ED. 2d 536 (1987) (no constitutional right to an attorney in habeas proceeding); See also 18 U.S.C. §

3599(a)(2) ("In any post-conviction proceeding under § 2254 of title 28 seeking to vacate or set aside a death sentence, any defendant who is or becomes financially unable to obtain adequate representation shall be entitled to the appointment of one or more than one attorney.")

Whether or not to appoint counsel is solely on the discretion of the federal judge. However, according to the Criminal Justice Act (COA), 18 U.S.C. §3006A(a)(2)(b) (quartz midpoint counsel when interest of justice require a petitioner is unable to afford the cost). moreover, the further appointment of counsel is demanded if the court holds an evidentiary hearing or is appropriate to grant discovery. See 2254 and 2255 Rule 8(c). The following is a list of cases, where it was held that an evidentiary hearing was appropriate.

1. Interest of Justice Appointment:

United States -V- Doe, 365 F.3d 150, 155 (2nd Cir. 2004);

(District Court has discretion to appoint counsel if interest of justice requires it).

Johnson -V- Chandler, 487 F.3d 1037, 1038 (7th Cir. 2007);

(Circuit Court benefited from defense counsel's representation of defendant in his appeal from denial of habeas petition Warren teen retroactive appointment of defense counsel in interest of justice).

Harris -V- Champion, 16 F.3d 1538, 1567 (10th Cir. 1994);

(District Court should consider appropriateness of appointing counsel for indigent petitioner when it decides to review in absence of exhaustion of state remedies).

Wyche -V- United States, 317 F.Supp.2d 1, 5-6 (Dist. Col. 2004);

(evaluating "the likelihood or success on the merits" along with the "complexity of the legal issues involved" in determining whether appointment is in the interest of justice).

Serrano -V- Fischer, 412 F.3d 292 (2nd Cir. 2005);

(appointment of counsel in the interest of justice under COA to assist with appeal or denial of his 2254 petition).

2. Appointment of Counsel to Assist with Evidentiary Hearing:

Bucci -V- United States, 662 F.3d 18, 34-35 (1st Cir. 2011);

(petitioner entitled to a new evidentiary hearing and appointment of counsel because prior evidentiary hearing for separate defendant, where petitioner had no counsel, resulted in judgment against both parties).

Graham -V- Portuondo, 506 F.3d 105, 106-08 (2nd Cir. 2008);

(petitioner entitled to a new hearing and appointment of counsel because District Court failed to appoint counsel at initial hearing).

<u>Armstrong -V- Kemna</u>, 534 F.3d 857, 868 n.5 (8th Cir. 2008);
(petitioner entitled to new hearing because District Court failed to appoint counsel at first evidentiary hearing).

<u>Shepherd -V- United States</u>, 253 F.3d 585, 587 (11th Cir. 2001);
(District Court is obligated to appoint counsel for a petitioner once it is determined that an evidentiary hearing is required to resolve the case/issue).

<u>McGriff -V- Dep't of Corr.</u>, 388 F.3d 1231, 1235 (11th Cir. 2003);
(failure to appoint counsel for 2254 petitioner was structural error necessitating a new hearing).

CHAPTER: 39

28 U.S.C. § 2255 HABEAS CORPUS RELIEF FOR FEDERAL PRISONERS:

When filing a § 2255 petition in the federal court, a pro se litigant must be absolutely sure that he follows the procedure, as set forth by the AEDPA. Below is the proper order that must be followed to make sure a habeas petitioner doesn't procedurally default himself from getting a full and fair review of his petition.

a. CUSTODY REQUIREMENT:

A federal District Court has jurisdiction to entertain a § 2255 motion only if a defendant is in custody under sentence of a federal court. See 28 U.S.C. § 2255(a). Moreover, whether a petitioner is in custody for § 2255 purposes is determined when the motion is filed. See Pola -V- United States, 778 F.3d 525, 529-30 (6th Cir. 2015) (petitioner in custody for § 2255 purposes when petitioner filed motion while in actual custody); Torzala -V- United States, 545 F.3d 517, 521 (7th Cir. 2008) (petitioner in custody for § 2255 despite no longer being in custody because petitioner was in custody when motion was filed); Ngyyen -V- United States, 114 F.3b 699, 703 (8th Cir. 1997) (petition are in custody for § 2255 purpose because in custody when proceeding instituted and federal conviction could have collateral consequences).

A petitioner is considered in custody under § 2255 when still subject to a period of supervised release. See Maleng -V- Cook, 490 U.S. 488, 491 (1989); Peck -V- United States, 73 F.3d 1220, 1224 n.5 (2nd Cir. 1995) (prisoner who had been paroled was "in custody" within § 2255), vacated or other grounds, 106 F.3d 450 (2nd Cir. 1997); United States -V- Essig, 10 F.3d 868, 970 n.5 (3rd Cir. 1993). Likewise, the custody requirement for a § 2255 petitioner is also satisfied if the prisoner is currently in custody under the judgment of a state court but is subject to future custody under the judgment of a federal District Court. See Rule 1(b). In short, the petitioner must be in some form of custody.

b. VENUE:

To have proper venue, a § 2255 motion must be filed in the District Court where the prisoner was sentenced. See 28 U.S.C. § 2255 Rule 4(a)(§ 2255 motions shall be presented to District Court judge who presided at movant's TRIAL AND SENTENCING); Moreno-Espada – V- United States, 666 F.3d 60, 64 (1st Cir. 2012) (§ 2255 Motion is petition to the sentencing court); Pack -V- Yasuff, 218 F.3d 448, 451 (5th Cir. 2000) (§ 2255 motions attack errors "at or prior to sentencing" and consequently "must be filed in the sentencing court."); In re Gregory, 181 F.3d 713, 714 (6th Cir. 1999) (§ 2255 motion contesting incarceration legality filed in sentencing court); Nichols -V- Symmes, 553 F.3d 647, 649 (8th Cir. 2009) (§ 2255 motion attacking validity of guilty plea must be filed in sentencing court); Muth -V- Pondren, 676 F.3d 815, 817 (9th Cir. 2012) (§2255 motion filed in custodial district required transfer to sentencing court for a hearing).

Sentencing court has been define as any court that has decided an issue affecting the terms of a petitioner sentence is a "sentencing court." See United States -V- Romera-Vilco, 850 F.2d 177, 178-79 (3rd Cir. 1988) (court that accepted defendant's guilty plea is sentencing court); United States -V- Flores, 616 F.2d 840, 842 (5th Cir. 1980) (court had accepted defendant's plea bargain in sentencing). It is well established that in order for a federal District Court to have proper jurisdiction to address a § 2255 motion, it has to also be the convicting/sentencing court.

c. ONE-YEAR FILING DEADLINE FOR § 2255

The Antiterrorism and Effective Death Penalty Act of 1996, Pub. L. No. 104-132. 110 Stat. 1214 ("AEDPA"), established a one-year period of limitation for the filing of § 2255 motion. The limitations period being from the latest of:

1. the date on which the judgment of conviction becomes final;

2. the date on which the impediment to making a motion created by government action in violation of the constitution or laws of the United states is removed, if the movant was prevented from making a motion by such government action;

3. the date on which the right asserted was initially recognized by the Supreme Court, if that right has been newly recognized by the Supreme Court and made retroactively applicable on collateral review; or

4. the date on which the facts supporting the claim or claims presented could have been discovered through the exercise of due diligence. 28 U.S.C. § 2255 (west Supp. 2018).

A judgment becomes final on the date the Supreme Court affirms the petitioner's conviction or denies a petition for certiorari or when the time for filing a petitioner for certiorari expires. See Clay -V- United States, 537 U.S. 522, 525 (2003) (conviction becomes final under § 2255 when time expires for filing a petition for certiorari contesting appellate court's for filing a petition for certiorari contesting appellate court's affirmation of conviction); Sepulveda -V- United States, 330 F.3d 55, 58 (1st Cir. 2003) (conviction of racketeering, witness intimidation, and possession of firearms as a convicted felon became final under § 2255 when Supreme Court denied certiorari); See Pena -V- United States, 534 F.3d 92, 93 n.3 (2nd Cir. 2008) (per curiam) (conviction of conspiracy to distribute heroin became final under § 2255 at deadline for filing certiorari petition). See Griffith -V- Kentucky, 479 U.S. 314, 93 L.ED. 2d 649, 107 S.CT. 708 (1987) (the Supreme Court stated that by final we mean a case in which a judgment of conviction has been rendered, the availability of appeal exhausted and the time for petition for certiorari denied) (citing United States -V- Johnson, 457 U.S. 537,

73 L.ED.2d 202, 102 S.CT. 2579 (1982)); <u>Corwin -V- Johnson</u>, 150 F.3d 467 (5th Cir. 1998) (the 1996 Anti-terrorism and Effective Death Penalty Act applies to habeas petition filed after AEDPA enacted); <u>Goodman -V- United States</u>, 151 F.3d 1335 (11th Cir. 1998) (one-year limitation period on 28 U.S.C. § 2255 motions to vacate, set-aside or correct sentence on defendant's conviction which became final prior to effective date of Antiterrorism and Effective Death Penalty Act, had one year form date of enactment of AEDPA, to file his § 2255 motion).

Before the one-year limitations period on a § 2255 motion may be tolled extraordinary circumstances must exist. See <u>Dodd -V- United States</u>, 545 U.S. 353, 357-58 (2005). The one year. Is a statute of limitations, not as jurisdictional bar, so courts have discretion to grant an extension of time. See <u>Holland -V- Florida</u>, 560 U.S. 631, 645 (2010).

In short, limitations imposed by the AEDPA apply to only cases filed after the act's effective date of April 24, 1996. See <u>Lindh -V- Murphy</u>, 521 U.S. 320, 327 (1997); see also <u>David -V- United States</u>, 134 F.3d 470, 473 n.1 (1st Cir. 1998) (explicitly applying Lindh exemption to § 2255); <u>Parker -V- United States</u>, 159 F.3d 1043, 1044 n.1 (7th Cir. 1998) (same); <u>Goodman -V- United States</u>, 151 F.3d 1335, 1337 (11th Cir. 1998) (same).

d. <u>MAILBOX RULE</u>:

A pro se § 2255 motion may be considered filed on the date it is deposited in the prison's internal mail system for forwarding to the District Court, provided the petitioner uses, if available, the prison system for recording legal mail. See e.g., <u>Morales-Rivera -V- United States</u>, 184 F.3d 109, 111 (1st Cir. 1999) (per curiam) (pro se § 2255 petition filed on date prisoner properly deposited it in prison mail system); <u>Starns -V- Andrews</u>, 524 F.3d 612, 616 (5th Cir. 2008) (pro se § 2255 petition filed on date prisoner submitted it to prison mailing system): <u>Towns -V- United States</u>, 190 F.3d 468, 469 (6th Cir. 1999) (pro se § 2255 petition filed on date prisoner delivered it to prison mailroom personnel); <u>United States -V- Harrison</u>, 469 F.3d 1216, 1217 (8th Cir. 2006) (pro se § 2255 petition filed on date deposited in prison mail system); <u>McCloud -V- Hooks</u>, 560 F.3d 1223, 1227 (11th Cir. 2009) (pro se § 2255 petition filed on date prisoner delivered it to prison mailing authorities). the law is clear in this area, that when a prisoner places his pleadings in the prison mailbox or handed to prison personnel, it is considered to be filed.

e. <u>EQUITABLE TOLLING</u>:

If a prisoner file his § 2255 motion timely, he may still be entitled to equitable tolling if he can show (1) that he has been pursuing his rights diligently, and (2) that some extraordinary circumstances stood in his way and prevented timely filing. Here are cases, where a petitioner was entitled to equitable tolling.

Ramos-Martinez -V- United States, 638 F.3d 315, 323 (1st Cir. 2011); (equitable tolling when paralegal failed to submit otherwise timely petition).

Harper -V- Ercole, 648 F.3d 132, 142 (2nd Cir. 2011); (equitable tolling when petitioners subjected to multiple surgeries during filing period).

United States -V- Wynn, 292 F.3d 226, 230 (5th Cir. 2002); (equitable tolling may be warranted if attorney deceived petitioner into believing timely § 2255 motion filed).

Solomon -V- United States, 467 F.3d 928, 933-35 (6th Cir. 2006); (equitable tolling allowed if petitioner lacked notice and constructive knowledge of deadline and responded not prejudiced by delay).

United States -V- Gabaldon, 522 F.3d 1121, 1126 (10th Cir. 2008); (equitable tolling permitted when petitioner's legal material confiscated shortly prior to filing deadline).

f. DISTRICT COURT PETITION PROCEDURE:

A motion filed pursuant to § 2255 must:

1. be substantially in the form of the model appended to the § 2255 rules;
2. specify all grounds for relief;
3. set forth in summary form the facts that justify relief;
4. state the relief requested;
5. be typed or written legibly
6. be signed by the petitioner; and
7. be filed in the office of the clerk of the district court along with two copies.

Once the district clerk agrees that all is in order, it will then be examined by the District Judge. See Rule 4(a). If a different judge presided at trial and sentencing, the motion must be examined by the judge who is in charge of the proceeding being attacked.

If the specified judge is unavailable however, the motion may be assigned to another judge from the district. See e.g., Gano -V- United States, 705 F.2d 1136, 1137 (9th Cir. 1983) (District Court judges appointment to another justice).

However, a District Court must construe pro se documents liberally. See Haines -V- Kerner, 404 U.S. 519, 520 (1972) (per curiam) (pro se complaint held to less stringent standard than formal papers drafted by lawyers); United States -V- Mosquera, 845 F.2d 1122, 1124-25 (1st Cir. 1988) (per curiam) (pro se § 2255 motion construed as not unduly conclusory); Marmolee -V- United States, 789 F.3d 66, 69 (2nd Cir. 2015) (pro se § 2255 motion construed liberally); United States -V- Otero, 502 F.3d 331, 334 (3rd Cir. 2007) (same); United States -V-

Torres, 163 F.3d 909, 910 n.5 (5th Cir. 1999) (same); see also United States -V-Ratliff, 999 F.2d 1023, 1026 (6th Cir. 1993) (same); Koons -V- United States, 630 F.3d 348, 355 n.2 (7th Cir. 2011) (same). After a pro se litigant has made it past summary dismissal, the District Judge will then order the United States Attorney to file an answer. See Rule 4(b).

Likewise, after the judge orders the United States Attorney to file his or her answer, he will also set a time for the answer to be filed, as well as describing the contents of what is to be filed. See Rule 5(a). This is what can be expected when a § 2255 motion is filed.

g. DETERMINING WHAT COGNIZABLE CLAIMS TO RAISE:

Unlike 2254, § 2255 provides for grounds that justify relief for a federal prisoner who challenges the fact or length of his or her confinement:

1. "that the sentence was imposed in violation of the constitution or laws of the United States;

2. that the court was without jurisdiction to impose such sentence;

3. that the sentence was in excess of the maximum authorized by law; or

4. that the sentence is otherwise subject to collateral attack."

Cognizable grounds for section 2255 motion are governed by § 2255(a), as shown by statute. Below are a list of cases that support cognizable grounds for a § 2255 motion.

Glover -V- United States, 531 U.S. 198, 203 (2001);

(claim that ineffective assistance of counsel led to sentencing error may be cognizable § 2255 constitutional violation).

Cuevas -V- Grondolsky, 671 F.3d 76, 78 (1st Cir. 2012);

(claim of extradition treaty violation cognizable under § 2255).

Morales -V- United States, 635 F.3d 39, 43 (2nd Cir. 2011);

(claim of inadequate representation cognizable under § 2255).

United States -V- Both, 432 F.3d 542, 550 (3rd Cir. 2005);

(claim of ineffective assistance of counsel allowed under § 2255).

United States -V- Brown, 155 F.3d 431, 433 (4th Cir. 1998);

(claim of double jeopardy violation cognizable under § 2255).

United States -V- Bokun, 73 F.3d 8, 12 (2nd Cir. 1995);

(challenge of court's jurisdiction generally available under § 2255).

Harris -V- United States, 149 F.3d 1304, 1307 (11th Cir. 1998);

(claim that trial court lacked jurisdiction to impose enhanced sentence cognizable under § 2255).

United States -V- Newbold, 791 F.3d 455, 456-61 (4th Cir. 2015);

(claim that armed Career Criminal Act sentence enhancement excessive and illegal after changing law cognizable under § 2255).

Narvaez -V- United States, 674 F.3d 621, 628 (7th Cir. 2011);
(claim that error in application of sentence guidelines cognizable under § 2255 as miscarriage of justice because post-conviction clarification in law made imposed sentence exceeds statutory maximum).

28 U.S.C. § 2255(a), the catch-all fourth category includes only assignment of error that reveal fundamental defects which . . . result in a complete miscarriage of justice, or irregularities that are inconsistent with the rudimentary demands of fair procedure. David -V- United States, 134 F.3d 470, 474 (1st Cir. 1998) (quoting Hill -V- United States, 368 U.S. 424, 428 (1962)).

Cuevas -V- United States, 778 F.3d 267, 271-72 (1st Cir. 2015) (sentence subject to collateral attack because prior convictions contributing to sentence calculation violated).

Now that you have determined what cognizable grounds to raise, check and make sure that none of your grounds are subject to procedural default.

h. PROCEDURAL DEFAULT:

District courts will not entertain a § 2255 motion if the petitioner did not raise a claim before trial, at trial, or direct appeal. See United States -V- Frady, 456 U.S. 152, 162-66 (1982). In order to overcome a procedural default petitioner must show both cause and prejudice for his failure to raise the claim in an earlier proceeding. See Frady, 456 U.S. at 167-68. Showing "cause" means establishing that the prisoner was impeded by "some objective factor external to the defense." Such as official interference making compliance with the procedural rule impractical, showing that a factual or legal basis for a claim was not reasonably available to counsel, or showing ineffective assistance of counsel. See McClesky -V- Zant, 499 U.S. 467, 493-94 (1991). The showing of cause and prejudice is not required, however, if:

1. the movement seeks § 2255 relief based on a constitutional violation that may have resulted in a fundamental miscarriage of justice, such as the conviction of an innocent person;

2. the government fails to object to the consideration of newly raised issues; or

3. the § 2255 motion raises certain constitutional claims that may be adequately addressed only on collateral review.

Occasionally, additional consideration will favor allowing other new claims to be raised on collateral review without a showing of cause and actual prejudice. See e.g., United States -V- Dula, 989 F.2d 772, 775-76 (5th Cir. 1993) (permitting Brady rule violation claim for failure to disclose evidence on collateral review without showing cause or prejudice because record on direct appeal inadequate to decide claim). to avoid all the above pitfalls of procedural default also known as the kiss of death, it is wise to raise all cognizable claims either on direct appeal, or to the District Court. Now, does a § 2255 petitioner have the right to the appointment of counsel?

i. APPOINTMENT OF COUNSEL:

The Sixth Amendment right to counsel does not attach to § 2255 proceedings. See Pa -V- Finley, 481 U.S. 551, 554 (1987) (no right to counsel in raising collateral attacks on conviction); Noe -V- United States, 601 F.3d 784, 792 (8th Cir. 2010) (same). However, the court in a non-capital case must appoint counsel when an evidentiary hearing is held. See Rule 8(c). See also Bucci -V- United States, 662 F.3d 18, 34 (1st Cir. 2011) (inmate entitled to appointment of counsel, for § 2255 evidentiary hearing under § 2255 Rule 8(c) if proven indigent); United States -V- Bendolph, 409 F.3d 155, 160 (3rd Cir. 2005) (same); United States -V- Vasquez, 7 F.3d 81, 84 (5th Cir. 1993) (same); Rauther -V- United States, 871 F.2d 693, 695 (7th Cir. 1989) (same); Greene -V- United States, 262 F.3d 715, 716-18 (8th Cir. 2001) (same); United States -V- Duarte-Higareda, 68 F.3d 369, 370 (9th Cir. 1995) (same); United States -V- Leopard, 170 F.3d 1013, 1015 (10th Cir. 1999) (same); Shepherd -V- United States, 250 F.3d 585, 587 (11th Cir. 2001) (same). Moreover, a § 2255 petitioner may be appointed counsel for utilization of discovery. See Rule 6(a). Likewise a District Court has consideration discretion in deciding whether to appoint counsel.

j. APPOINTMENT OF COUNSEL FOR MOVANT ON §2255:

See 28 U.S.C. § 2255(g) ("Appointment of counsel under [§ 2255] shall be governed by section 3006A of title 18"); 18 U.S.C. § 3006A(a)(2)(B) (court may furnish council when interest of justice so require a petitioner financially unable to afford council); See Rule 8(c) (Court may furnish council, pursuant to statutory authority, "at any stage" if "interest of justice so require"); See United States -V- Mala, 7 F.3d 1058, 1063-64 (1st Cir. 1993) (council appointed for petitioner if § 2255 relief sought because appellant showed fair likelihood of success on constitutional claim, claim was factually complex and legally intricate, and facts were underdeveloped and appellant hampered by indigence and incarcerated); United States -V- Barnes, 662 F.3d 777, 780 (D.C. Cir. 1980) (council appointed left to court's discretion). Basically a § 2255 movant, is not completely estopped from having counsel appointed to him, it just depends on the circumstances and the facts of the case. Remember, NO two cases are alike.

k. SUCCESSIVE § 2255 MOTION:

Availability of relief under § 2255 through second or successive motion is severely limited period in District Court may hear a second or successive § 2255 motion only if a three-judge panel of the appropriate Court of Appeals certifies that the motion relies on either: (1) newly discovered evidence that, if proven and viewed in light of the evidence as a whole, would be sufficient to establish that no reasonable factfinder would have found the movant guilty of the offence, or (2) a new rule of constitutional law, mean retroactive to cases on collateral review by the Supreme Court, that was previously unavailable on direct review. See 28 U.S.C. § 2255(h)(1)(2). See also United States -V- Sevilla, 770 F.3d 1, 12 (1st Cir. 2014) (second or successive § 2255 motion required appellate permission for District Court to consider); Whab -V- United States, 408 F.3d 116, 118 (2nd Cir. 2005) (same); In re Turner, 267 F.3d 225, 227 (3rd Cir. 2001) (same); United States -V- McRae, 793 F.3d 392, 397 (4th Cir. 2015) (same); in re Lampton, 667 F.3d 585, 590 n.22 (5th Cir. 2012) (same); United States -V- Carter, 500 F.3d 486, 490 (6th Cir. 2007) (same); Phillips -V- United States, 668 F.3d 433, 436 (7th Cir. 2012) (same); United States -V- Lee, 792 F.3d 1021, 1023 (8th Cir. 2015) (same); Ezell -V- United States, 778 F.3d 762, 765 (same); United States -V- Williams, 790 F.3d 1059, 1067-69 (10th Cir. 2015) (same); United States -V- Holt, 417 F.3d 1172, 1175 (11th Cir. 2005) (same); United Sates -V- Arrington, 763 F.3d 12, 23 (D.C. Cir. 2014) (same).

However, if the second or successive § 2255 motion is for an out of time appeal, it will be allowed without asking for permission from the Circuit Court of appeals. See Carranza -V- United States, 792 F.3d 237, 238 (2nd Cir. 2015) (second or successive § 2255 motion did not require appellate permission because motion only sought to restore direct-appeal rights and did not challenge sentence's legality); Clark -V- United States, 764 F.3d 653, 658-59 (6th Cir. 2014) (second 2255 motion does not require appellate permission if filed while initial motion still pending and should be construed as motion to amend); United States -V- Sellner, 773 F.3d 927, 930-32 (8th Cir. 2014) (same).

A movant filing a second or successive § 2255 motion can prevail if he is raising a new rule of constitutional law. See Dodd -V- United States, 545 U.S. 353, 359 (2005) ("[A]n applicant who files a second or successive motion [to vacate] seeking to take advantage of a new rule of constitutional law will be time barred" except in rare cases where court announces, "new rule of constitutional law and makes it retroactive within one year."). See Allen -V- Buss, 558 F.3d 657, 661 (7th Cir. 2009) (movant entitled to protection of new rule prohibiting execution of mentally retarded persons because court previously stated holding would apply retroactively). Filing a second or successive § 2255 motion, while demanding, is not impossible to have granted. It depends on the same facts and circumstances of your case, and not every case is the same, it is important to remember that.

l. FILING CERTIFICATE OF APPEALIBILITY (COA):

Final orders issued pursuant to § 2255 are appealable only if a judge issues a certificate of appealability requirement applies only to appeals filed under AEDPA's effective date of April 24, 1996. See Slack -V- McDaniels, 529 U.S. 473, 482 (2000) (effective date of § 2253(c) applies to date petitioner appeals court denial of habeas petition, not date habeas petition originally filed with District Court); see e.g., Gratzer -V- Mahoney, 397 F.3d 686, 689 (9th Cir. 2005) (certificate of appealability unnecessary for appeal filed prior to effective date of AEDPA); Lindh -V- Murphy, 521 U.S. 320, 326-27 (1997) (amendments to habeas statute do not apply to state inmate's noncapital case pending at time amendments became effective).

A Circuit Judge may grant a certificate of appealability "only if the applicant has made a substantial showing of the denial of a constitutional right," and the judge must indicate in the certificate which specific issue or issues satisfy this showing. See 28 U.S.C. § 2253(c)(2)-(3); see also Slack, 529 U.S. at 484 (Circuit Judge should issue certificate of appealability if debatable that habeas petition states valid constitutional claim and district court's procedural ruling was incorrect); See United States -V- Surratt, 797 F.3d 240, 261 (4th Cir. 2015) (certificate of appealability not warranted because petitioner did not show substantial deprivation of constitutional right).

Moreover, if a District Court denies a § 2255 petition on procedural grounds, a Circuit Judge must also consider whether "jurists of reason" could disagree with the procedural ruling. See Miller-El -V- Cockrell, 537 U.S. 322, 327 (2003); Slack, 529 U.S. at 484; ("[P]etitioner must demonstrate that reasonable jurists would find the district court's assessment of the constitutional claim debatable or wrong."). The standard for obtaining a COA is pretty clear. Likewise, any appeal from the denial of a § 2255 motion must be made within 60 days (60). See Fed.R.App. 4(a)(1); See also United States -V- Garcdia-Machado, 845 F.2d 492, 493 (5th Cir. 1988) (per curiam) (appeal of denial of § 2255 motion dismissed because not filed within 60 days of judgment as required by Fed.R.App. P. 4(a)(1); Morales -V- Bezy, 499 F.3d 668, 671 (7th Cir. 2007) (same); United States -V- Williams, 790 F.3d 1059, 1077 n.14 (10th Cir. 2015) (same); United States -V- Palmer, 296 F.3d 1135, 1142-43 (D.C. Cir. 2002) (same). Moreover, the time to file an appeal from the denial of a § 2255 motion begins on the date the order is signed. See Williams -V- United States, 984 F.2d 28, 29-30 (2nd Cir. 1993).

CHAPTER: 40

OBTAINING DISCOVERY

It is not impossible for a federal or state prisoner to obtain discovery. Pursuant to Rule 6 of the rules governing section 2254 and 2255 cases if a petitioner can show good cause and the court exercises his or her discretion to allow discovery. Federal Rules of Civil Procedure, Rule 26(a) through 36 provides a wide range of discovery devices available which includes but not limited to: "Depositions, production of documents or other physical materials, physical and mental examinations, request for admission and interrogatories, permission to enter upon land or other property for inspection or other purposes. The court may appoint counsel for indigent prisoners if necessary for effective utilization of discovery." See 18 U.S.C. § 3006A(g). See Bracy -V- Gramley, 520 U.S. 899, 908-09, 138 L.ED.2d 97 (1997); Toney -V- Gammon, 79 F.3d 693 (8th Cir. 1995) (A petitioner claiming systematic discrimination in formulation of juries was entitled to supplements record . . . with deposition of official custodian of county's jury list); Bader -V- Warden, 488 F.3d 483, 486 (1st Cir. 2007); ("in civil matters including habeas, evidentiary proceedings are appropriate only where the party bearing the burden of proof on an element starts with enough evidence to create a genuine issue of fact; Otherwise, summary judgment is proper); Rice -V- Clark, 923 F.2d 117 (8th Cir. 1991) (state's failure to provide defense counsel with type of emergency 911-phone call, which lured police officer to his death, and did not violate due process); United States -V-Roane, 373 F.3d 382, 402-08 (*4th Cir. 2004) ("discovery is warranted where specific allegations before the court show reasons to believe that the petitioner may, if the facts are fully developed, be able to demonstrate that he is - - - entitled to relief); See also Reed -V- Quarterman, 504 F.3d 465, 471-72 (5th Cir. 2007) (same); Rice -V- Clark, 923 F.2d 117 (8th Cir. 1991) (habeas petitioner was granted discovery to ascertain whether the FBI performed a voiceprint analysis of the telephone caller's voice because of the statement by the assistant chief of police).

CHAPTER: 41

ENTITLED TO OBTAIN TRANSCRIPTS

Indigent § 2255 petitioners are entitled to free transcripts of prior proceedings such as arraignment, trial sentencing, and other proceedings pursuant to 28 U.S.C. § 753(f) (authorizing free transcripts for § 2255 petitioners granted in forma pauperis status upon certification by the trial judge . . . that the suit . . . is not frivolous and that the transcript is needed to decide the issue presented by the suit."). However, a petitioner is not entitled to free transcripts of prior state proceedings are unavailable via § 753(f). See also <u>Russell -V- Jones</u>, 886 F.2d 149 (8th Cir. 1989). Moreover, a petitioner may not file for his/her transcripts until after motion pursuant to § 2255 has been filed. <u>United States -V- Horvath</u>, 157 F.3d 131, 132 (2nd Cir. 1998) (per curiam); <u>Boyd -V- Newland</u>, 467 F.3d 1139, 1150-51 (9th Cir. 2006) (indigent petitioners entitled to voir dire transcripts to develop plausible claim). However, failure to provide the transcript does not violate due process of law. See <u>United States -V- MacCollom</u>, 426 U.S. 317, 323-26 (1979) (court's failure to grant indigent federal prisoner unconditional right to obtain trial transcripts for § 2255 proceeding did not violate due process or equal protection of law).

As mentioned above, just because you're indigent doesn't mean you have the right to free transcripts. See <u>Matthews -V- Price</u>, 83 F.3d 323, 334 (10th Cir. 1998) (free transcript denial justified because transcript did not provide useful evidence for § 2255 claim). See <u>United States -V- Silker</u>, 751 F.2d 477, 491 (2nd Cir. 1984) (claims must not be frivolous); <u>Walker -V- People Express Airlines, Inc.</u>, 888 F.2d 598, 600 (3rd Cir. 1989) (citing to requirements of § 753(f)); <u>Hoover -V- United States</u>, 416 F.2d 431 (8th Cir. 1969) ("where the petitioner seeking a transcript had stated the reasons why he believes his conviction is contrary to law and a transcript is indispensable to the filing of a motion, then it may be granted at government expense."). See <u>Hansen -V- United States</u>, 956 F.2d 245, 248 (11th Cir. 1998) (prisoners have a right of access to court files pertaining to their underlying criminal conviction, but only after the filing of the petitioner and upon a showing that access is necessary to the resolution of an issue or issues).

Only one court has held that a petitioner can obtain the record before filing his 2255 motion, in order to see the facts to know exactly what to raise in his motion. See <u>United States ex rel. Davidson -V- Wilkinson</u>, 618 F.2d 1215, 1219 (7th Cir. 1980). It is important to obtain the transcripts of any federal court proceedings because the burden of proof always lies on the petitioner. Therefore, upon proper request pursuant to 28 U.S.C. § 753(b), the District Court should promptly mail the record to the prisoner as long as all the safeguards are met. See <u>Rush -V- United States</u>, 559 F.2d 455, 459 (7th Cir. 1997).

CHAPTER: 42

RIGHT TO BAIL ON HABEAS CORPUS

It has long been held that Federal District Court Judges have wide latitude when it comes to granting bail in § 2254 or § 2255 proceedings, while awaiting the decision of the Court of Appeals. See <u>Cherek -V- United States</u>, 767 F.2d 335, 337 (7th Cir. 1985); <u>Bowen -V- Maynard</u>, 799 F.2d 595, 613-14 n.12 (10th Cir. 1986); <u>Mapp -V- Reno</u>, 241 F.3d 221, 226 (2nd Cir. 2001); <u>Baker -V- Sard</u>, 410 F.2d 1342, 1343 (D.C. Cir. 1969).

Moreover, bail is to be granted only in extraordinary circumstances. See <u>Landano -V- Rafferty</u>, 970 F.2d 1230, 1240 (3rd Cir. 1992) (extraordinary circumstances not shown); <u>Calley -V- Callaway</u>, 496 F.2d 701, 702 (5th Cir. 1974) (must have meritorious claim in extraordinary circumstances); <u>Argo -V- United States</u>, 505 F.2d 670 (1st Cir. 1982) (no extraordinary circumstances found).

The cases presented herein, may make it seem impossible to obtain bail in a habeas corpus proceeding, but it isn't, it depends on the circumstances and the facts of the case. Remember, no two cases are alike.

CHAPTER: 43

RULE 60 MOTIONS

A motion pursuant to Rule 60 of the Federal Rules of Civil Procedure can be used to reopen a § 2254 or § 2255 proceeding, but only in limited circumstances. Motions that seek "to add a new ground for relief," or attack in "court's previous resolution of a claim on the merits" are not permitted and will be treated as a second or successive petition. See Gonzales -V- Crosby, 545 U.S. 524, 162 L.ED.2d 480 (2005). Moreover, a Rule 60(b) motion must "confine itself" to the first federal habeas petition and challenge only "it's a non-merit aspect." e.g., a determination that a claim was time barred or procedurally defaulted, "of the first federal habeas proceedings." Id. at 534. See also e.g., Sheppard -V- Robinson, 807 F.3d 815, 818 (6th Cir. 2015); Post -V- Bradshaw, 422 F.3d 419, 424 (6th Cir. 2005) (Rule 60(b) motion that seeks to advance newly discovered evidence concerning claims the District Court previously considered and dismissed on substantiative ground is second or successive petition); Munoz -V- United States, 331 F.3d 151, 152 (1st Cir. 2009) (Rule 60(b) motion treated as a second and successive habeas petition because it mainly challenged constitutionality of petitioners underlying conviction); Sanders -V- Norris, 529 F.3d 787, 790 (8th Cir. 2008) (Rule 60(b) motion that seeks "leave to present newly discovered evidence . . . in support of a claim previously denied" must be treated as successive); Jones -V- Ryan, 733 F.3d 825, 835-37 (9th Cir. 2013) (same); In re Pickard, 681 F.3d 1201, 1206(10th Cir. 2012) (Rule 60(b) motion treated a second or successive habeas petition because Brady and Giglio claims asserts basis for relief from underlying conviction); United States-V- Lee, 792 F.3d 1021, 1023 (8th Cir. 2015) (Rule 60(b) motion treated as second or successive habeas petition because petitioner challenged district court's decision on the merits).

However, if a Rule 60(b) motion that attacks only a "defect in the integrity of the federal habeas proceedings," or that challenge a procedural ruling that precluded a merits determination will not be treated as second or successive, see Gonzales, 545 U.S. at 538; Harris -V- United States, 367 F.3d 74, 80 (2nd Cir. 2004) (Rule 60(b) motion not treated as second or successive habeas petition, and so considered on merits, because motion attacked integrity of petitioners habeas proceeding); Norris -V- Brooks, 794 F.3d 401, 403 n.2 (3rd Cir. 2015) (Rule 60(b) motion not treated as second or successive habeas petition because motion merely asserted previous ruling, which precluded merits determination, was erroneous); Adams -V- Thaler, 679 F.3d 312, 319(5th Cir. 2012) (Rule 60(b) motion not treated as second and successive habeas petition because petitioner, challenged District Court determination that claims were procedurally defaulted); Canales -V- Quarterman, 507 F.3d 884, 887 (5th Cir. 2007) ("Rule 60(b) motion is not to be treated as a success of habeas petition if the motion attacks a defect in the integrity of the federal habeas proceedings and does not raise a new ground for relief or attack the district court's resolution of a claim on the merits"); <u>Phelps -V- Alameida</u>, 569 F.3d 1120 (9th Cir. 2009) (granting a Rule 60(b)(6) relief to habeas petitioner whose claims were erroneously time barred).

A certificate of appealability (COA) is required before petitioner may appeal the denial of a Rule 60 motion. <u>West -V- Schneiter</u>, 485 F.3d 393 (9th Cir. 2007) (COA required to appeal the denial of Rule 60(b) motion that challenged procedural ruling); <u>Reid -V- Angelone</u>, 369 F.3d 363, 369 n.2 (4th Cir. 2004) (requiring a COA for appeal from Rule 60(b) orders in habeas cases). The supreme court's decision in <u>Harbison -V- Bell</u>, 556 U.S. 180, 183-85 (2009), has changed the rules when it comes to procedurally defaulting a claim. In Harbison, the court basically ruled that a ruling on a final order is all that may be appealed, and that a Rule 60 motion that attacks a procedural ruling that didn't address the merits of the case is not a "final order that disposes of the merits" of a case. Therefore, a COA, under such circumstances, should not be required. With that in mind, be sure to research the issue raised pursuant to a 60(b) motion before filing for a COA, to make sure that issue is ripe for appeal.

CHAPTER: 44

WRIT OF AUDITA QUERELA & ERROR CORAM NOBIS

The all-writs act does not itself confer any subject matter jurisdiction, but rather some only allows a federal court to issue writs "in aid of" its existing jurisdiction. See Clinton -V- Goldsmith, 526 U.S. 529, 534, 119 S.CT. 1538, 143 L.ED.2d 720 (1999); Syngenta Crop Prot. Inc -V- Henson, 537 U.S. 28, 31, 125 S.CT. 366, 254 L.ED. 2d 358 (2002); See also In re Arunachalam, 812 F.3d 290, 292 (3rd Cir. 2010) (per curiam).

Therefore, a court has subject matter jurisdiction over an application for an all-writs act order only when it has subject matter jurisdiction over the underlying order that the all-writs act order is intended to effectuate. Additionally, a federal court may only issue an all-writs act order "as may be necessary or appropriate to effectuate and prevent the frustration of orders it has previously issued in its exercise or jurisdiction otherwise obtained." United States -V- N.Y. Tel. Co., 434 U.S. 159, 172, 98 S.CT. 364, 54 L.ED.2d 376 (1977).

WRIT OF AUDITA QUERELA:

Audtia Querela, is Latin for "the complaint having been heard," was an ancient writ used to act enforcement of a judgment after it was rendered. Black's Law Dictionary, 126 (7th ed. 1999). The common law writ was typically employed by judgment debtor in a civil case against the execution of a judgment, because of some defense or discharge arising subsequent to the rendition of the judgment or the issue of the execution. See Gonzales -V- Sec'y for the Dept. of Corr., 360 F.3d 1253, 1289 (11th Cir. 2004) (Soflat J. Dissenting). At this time there are no reported appellate decisions were a prisoner has been granted relief with respect to an Audita Querela outside of the U.S. Immigration process. The reasons for this is because the writ of audita querela was abolished, in the civil context by the federal rules of Civil Procedure. See Fed.R.Civ.P. 60(b). the courts have yet to address the writs continued applicability in the criminal context.

WRIT OF ERROR CORAM NOBIS:

The writ of error Coram nobis is an "extraordinary remedy," United States -V- Morgan, 346 U.S. 502, 511, 74 S.CT. 247, 252, 98 L.ED. 248 (1958), available to a petitioner no longer in custody, who seeks to vacate his conviction in circumstances where "the petitioner can demonstrate that he is suffering civil disabilities as a consequence of the criminal conviction, and that the challenged error is of sufficient magnitude to justify the extraordinary relief." See United States -V- Marcello, 876 F.3d 1147, 1154 (5th Cir. 1989) (citations omitted). Moreover, the remedy Coram nobis "should issue to correct only error which result in a complete miscarriage of justice." Id., (Citing Morgan, 346 U.S. at 512, 74 S.CT. at 253). However, the standard for Coram nobis relief can be more "demanding" than the causes and prejudice standard for habeas corpus relief under 28 U.S.C. § 2255.

Likewise, a writ of error Coram nobis "will issue only when no other remedy is available and when 'sound reasons exist for failing to seek appropriate earlier relief.'" United States -V- Dyer, 136 F.3d 417, 422 (5th Cir. 1998) (quoting Morgan, 346 U.S. at 512, 74 S.CT. at 247); See United States -V- Esogbue, 357 F.3d 532, 535 (5th Cira. 2004) (an assertion that he would have been unable to satisfy the stringent standards for filing a successive § 2255 motion while he was in custody is not such a "sound reason.") See Godoski -V- United States, 304 F.3d 761, 763 (7th Cir. 2002) ("Coram nobis is a common law writ, and it is entirely inappropriate for the judiciary to invoke the common law to override limitations enacted by Congress, such as the limitations in § 2255"), cert. denied 537 U.S. 1211, 123 S.CT. 1304, 154 L.ED. 2d 1059 (2003); Matus-Leva -V- United States, 287 F.3d 761 (9th Cir. 2008) ("a petitioner may not resort to Coram nobis merely because he has failed to meet the AEDPA's gatekeeping requirements. To hold otherwise would circumvent the AEDPA's overall purpose of expediting the presentation of claims in federal court and enable prisoners to bypass the limitations and successive petitions provisions"), cert. denied, 537U.S. 1022, 123 S.CT. 544, 154 L.ED. 431 (2002).

Courts have held that the writ of error Coram nobis is unavailable while incarcerated. Flemming -V- United States, 146 F.3d 88, 89-90 (2nd Cir. 1998) (explaining that a writ of error Coram nobis is "essentially a remedy of last resort for petitioners who are no longer in custody pursuant to a criminal conviction and therefore cannot pursue direct review or collateral relief by means of a writ of habeas corpus"). In re Daniels, 203 Fed. Appx. 442 (*4th Cir. 2006) (coram nobis unavailable while incarcerated); Blanton -V- United States, 94 F.3d 227, 231 (6th Cir. 1996) (same); United States -V- Torres, 282 F.3d 1241, 1245 (10th Cir. 2002) (same).

The Coram nobis is not dead in federal courts, despite the enactment of the AEDPA, courts usually recognize common law writs when necessary. See United States -V- Ayala, 894 F.2d 425, 428 (D.C. Cir. 1990), see also United States -V- Kimberlin, 675 F.2d 866, 869 (7th Cir. 1982) (noting that federal courts may recognize common law writs in a criminal context when "necessary to plug a gap in the system of federal post-conviction remedies"). The authority of federal courts to recognize common law post-conviction remedies to the all-writs act, 28 U.S.C. § 1651 is governed by the Supreme Court's decision in United States -V- Morgan, 346 U.S. 502, 74 S.CT. 247, 98 L.ED. 248 (1954).

CHAPTER: 45

SENTENCE REDUCTION PURSUANT TO FED.R.CRIM.P. 35(B): FEDERAL PRISONERS ONLY

Rule 35 of the Federal Rules of Criminal Procedure permits a District Court to reduce a sentence to reflect the defendant subsequent substantial assistance in the investigation or prosecution of another criminal. See Fed.R.Crim.P. 35(b); United States -V- Clawson, 650 F.3d 530, 537 (4th Cir. 2011) (sentence reduction for substantial assistance under Rule 35(b) invalid because court granted motion based on findings unrelated to defendants substantial assistance); United States -V- Chapman, 532 F.3d 625, 630-31 (7th Cir. 2008) (sentence reduction for substantial assistance under Rule 35(b) valid); United States -V- Davis, 679 F.3d 190, 195-96 (4th Cir. 2012) (court may consider factors unrelated to defendant's substantial assistance when determining extent of sentence reduction under Rule 35(b)); see also United States -V- Anonymous, 629 F.3d 68, 76 (1st Cir. 2010) (sentence reduction for substantial assistance under Rule 35(b) valid despite falling short of state's full recommendation for downward revision); United States -V- Jenkins, 105 F.3d 411, 412 (8th Cir. 1997) (plea agreement promised to file Rule 35 motion in exchange for substantial assistance is enforceable).

A sentencing court may only consider factors relevant to a defendant substantial assistance in weighing whether to grant a Rule 35(b) motion; However, the court may consider § 3553(a) factors unrelated to a defendant's substantial assistance when determining the extent of a reduction. See e.g., United States -V- Davis, 679 F.3d 190, 195-96 (4th Cir. 2012) (court may consider factors unrelated to defendant substantial assistance when determining extent of sentence reduction under Rule 35(b)); , 636 F.3d 803, 816-17 (6th Cir. 2011) (same); United States -V- Rublee, 655 F.3d 835, 839 (8th Cir. 2011) (same); United States -V- Tadio, 663 F.3d 1042, 1052 (9th Cir. 2011) (same).

Moreover, a prison sentence also may be reduced for extraordinary or compelling reasons, but only on a motion by the Bureau of prisons. See 18 U.S.C. § 3582(c)(1)(A)(2006). However, reduction of sentence under this provision is wholly separate from rule 35. The Senate Judiciary Committee explained that this provision applies to the unusual case in which the defendant circumstances are so changed, such as by terminal illness, that continued confinement would be inequitable. This provision may be applied regardless of the length of sentence. This type of reduction or release is also known as a compassionate release. See S. Rep. No. 98-225 (1984)., reprinted in 1984 U.S.C.C.A.N. 3182, 3304.

Therefore, there are two ways a federal prisoner may be granted a sentence reduction.

CHAPTER: 46

28 U.S.C. § 2255 DISTINGUISHED FROM 28 U.S.C. § 2241: FEDERAL PRISONERS ONLY

First off, a § 2241 petition is filed in the jurisdiction where the prisoner is held, whereas a § 2255 petition is filed in the jurisdiction where the prisoner was tried or sentence. It is important to know that the motions are not interchangeable.

The "saving clause" of § 2255 forbids courts from entertaining habeas petitions under § 2241 from prisoners "authorized to apply for relief" under § 2255 unless § 2255 is "inadequate or ineffective." See U.S.C. § 2255(e).

However, section 2255 is not "inadequate or ineffective" merely because a petitioner cannot satisfy procedural requirements for filing a second or successive motions or fails to meet § 2255's one-year period of limitations. See United States -V- Barrett, 178 F.3d 34, 50 (1st Cir. 1999). Thompson -V- Choinski, 525 F.3d 205, 209 (2nd Cir. 2008); several circuits have held that § 2255 is "inadequate or ineffective" when its limitations on second or successive motions preclude a prisoner from challenging a sentence imposed for conduct rendered non-criminal by Supreme Court decision issued after the prisoners initial § 2255 motion. See Triestman -V- United States, 124 F.3d 361, 380 (2nd Cir. 1997) (§ 2255 "inadequate or ineffective" and § 2241 petition allowable when Supreme Court retroactive interpretation of statute overturned well-established circuit interpretation, rendering prisoners offence nonexistent); In re Jones, 226 F.3d 328, 334 (4th Cir. 2000) (§ 2255 "inadequate or ineffective" if (1) prisoner convicted under settled law; (2) subsequent to prisoners direct appeal and first § 2255 motion, substantiative law changed that conduct for which prisoner was convicted deemed not criminal; and (3) prisoner cannot satisfy gatekeeping provisions of § 2255 because new rule is not one of constitutional law).

Most circuits have read "inadequate or ineffective" very narrowly, and only prisoners claiming actual innocence had been allowed to invoke § 2241. See United States -V- Fields, 761 F.3d 443, 478-80 (5th Cir. 2014) (§ 2255 not "inadequate or ineffective" when prisoner's claim of actual innocence when based on speculative and conclusory evidence and reasonable jurists would not debate the district court's holding).

Finally, a § 2255 motion is the proper means to challenge the validity or lawfulness of a conviction. Whereas, a § 2241 petition is the proper means to challenge the execution of a sentence or confinement that is not the result of a criminal court's judgement. See Muniz -V- Sabol, 517 F.3d 29, 34-35 (1st Cir. 2008) (§ 2241 claim proper because prisoner's challenge to delay transfer sought relief from manner sentence executed); Thompson -V- Choinski, 525 F.3d 205, 209 (2nd Cir. 2008) (§ 2241 claim proper because prisoner challenged conditions of confinement). Therefore, § 2241 petitions are primarily open to prisoners challenging unlawful condition of treatment or confinement. See Nichols -V-

<u>Symmes</u>, 553 F.3d 647, 649 (8th Cir. 2009). Or aliens detained by U.S. Citizenship and Immigration Services. See <u>Zadvydas -V- Davis</u>, 533 U.S. 678, 687-88 (2001), and prisoners incarcerated by the U.S. military. See <u>Boumediene -V- Bush</u>, 553 U.S. 723, 771 (2008); see also <u>Munaf -V- Geren</u>, 553 U.S. 674, 685 (2008) (U.S. citizens in custody of U.S. military when part of multinational forces may file § 2241 petitions but may not prevent transfer to foreign in some circumstances).

Prisoners must also use a § 2241 petition to challenge actions by the U.S. Parole Commission in connection with their sentence. See <u>United States -V- Addonizio</u>, 442 U.S. 178, 190 (1979) (Parole Commission's actions "do not retroactively affect" validity of final judgment and thus "do not provide a basis for a collateral attack" pursuant to § 2255".).

Section 2255 motions are subject to the Rules Governing Section § 2255 adoption. The Procedural Rules for § 2255 motions differ from the rules governing federal prisoner's habeas corpus petitions under § 2241. See Id. at Rule 1 (lack of filing fee, automatic availability of files related to judgment, broader discovery, no extension of time of appeal, applicability of federal criminal rules differentiates § 2255 motion from habeas petition).

APPENDIX – A NOTICE OF APPEAL:

IN THE UNITED STATES DISTRICT COURT
FOR   THE   _____   DISTRICT   OF

_____ DIVISION

UNITED STATES OF AMERICA,   Civil   No.

_____

Respondent,   Criminal No. _____
Vs.

_____,

Petitioner.

NOTICE OF APPEAL

Notice is hereby given that (Your name here), the petitioner hereby appeals to the United states Court of Appeals for the _____circuit from the final judgment (of whatever motion, petition, or order of the court which you're appealing to), entered for record in the above action on the _____ day of _____, 20 _____.

Respectfully submitted,
(Your Signature) _____
(Your name) _____
(Your address) _____
(City, State, & Zip Code) _____
APPENDIX – B CERTIFICATE OF SERVICE:

CERTIFICATE OF SERVICE

I HEREBY CERTIFY that a true and correct copy of this foregoing instrument has been mailed postage prepaid on this _____ day of _____, 20 _____, to the __(opposing party),__ at ____(opposing Party's address),__ by depositing same in the mailbox at _____ institution.

/s/ _____
(Your Name)

APPENDIX – B MOTION FOR LEAVE TO PROCEED ON APPEAL IN FORMA PAUPERIS:

IN THE UNTED STATES DISTRICT COURT

FOR THE _____ DISTRICT OF _____

DIVISION

UNITED STATES OF AMERICA,   Civil   No.

_____

Respondent,   Criminal No. _____

Vs.

_____,

Petitioner.

MOTION FOR LEAVE TO PROCEED ON APPEAL IN FORMA PAUPERIS

NOW INTO COURT comes _____, the petitioner, appearing through pro se representation and respectfully moves this Honorable Court for leave to proceed on appeal through in forma pauperis from the judgement entered on _____, without prepayment of costs and fees, and without giving security, therefore.

An affidavit in Support of this Motion to Proceed on Appeal in Forma Pauperis is attached hereto and made part of this motion by reference herein.

Respectfully submitted,

(Your Name) _____

PRO SE RESPRESENTATION

(Your Address) _____

(CITY, STATE & ZIP CODE)

APPENDIX – C AFFIDAVIT IN SUPPORT OF MOTION TO PROCEED ON IN FORMA PAUPERIS:

IN THE UNTED STATES DISTRICT COURT
FOR THE _____ DISTRICT OF _____
DIVISION
_____

UNITED STATES OF AMERICA,   Civil   No.
_____

Respondent,   Criminal No. _____
Vs.

_____,
Petitioner.
_____
AFFIDAVIT IN SUPPORT OF MOTION TO PROCEED ON APPEAL IN FORMA
PAUPERIS
_____

    I, _____ being duly sworn, depose and says that:

    1.   I state that because of my poverty I am unable to pay the costs of said proceeding or to give security therefore; that I believe I am entitled to redress; in that the issues which I desired to raise on appeal will entitle a reversal of the judgment mentioned on the following grounds;

    2.   [Specify the proposed grounds for appeal].

    3.   [List and describe all of (Appellant's) monthly wages, salary, and address of employer, income within past year; total amount and value of cash, checking, savings and/or other bank accounts, stocks, and assets, names and relationship of your dependents].

    4.   I _____, therefore request leave to prosecute the proposed appeal through in forma pauperis status.

    I understand that a false statement in this affidavit will subject me to the penalties of perjury.

    I declare under penalty of perjury pursuant to Title 28 United States Code, Section 1746, and 18 United States Code, Section 162, that the foregoing information contained herein this affidavit is true and correct.

    Executed at _____ on this _____ day of _____, 20 _____.

APPENDIX – D STATEMENT OF INSTITUTIONAL ACCOUNTS:

Prisoner's name _____

I hereby certify that on this _____ day of _____, 20 _____, this prisoner had a total of $ _____ in his/her institutional account(s). I further certify that the amounts listed below are correct.

1. Average monthly deposits to the prisoner's account(s) for the 6-month period immediately preceding the filing of this action:

$ _____ x 20% = $ _____

I further certify that the above amount(s), a copy of which is attached hereto.

_____

Authorized Prison Official

_____

Title

APPENDIX – E MOTION FOR APPOINTMENT OF COUNSEL:

MOTION FOR APPOINTMENT OF COUNSEL

NOW INTO COURT comes _____, the petitioner appearing through pro se representation and respectfully moves this Honorable Court to appoint counsel for the purpose of representing the petitioner's (describe the proceedings which you desire counsel represent you in), pursuant to Title 18 U.S.C. § 3006A.

Wherefore, the petitioner _____, prays this Honorable Court will appoint counsel to represent (him/her) in the above action.

Respectfully submitted,

/s/ _____

(Your name)

(DOC #)

(Your Prison Unit)

(City, State, & Zip Code)

APPENDIX — F MOTION FOR LEAVE TO AMEND 28 U.S.C. § 2554 HABEAS CORPUS PETITION:

MOTION FOR LEAVE TO AMEND 28 U.S.C. § 2254 habeas corpus petition

---

    NOW INTO COURT comes _____, the petitioner, appearing through pro se representation and respectfully moves this Honorable Court for leave to file an amendment to his U.S.C. § 2254 habeas corpus petition, pursuant to Federal Rules of Civil Procedure, Rule 15(a), leave to amend shall be freely given when justice so requires.

    A memorandum brief in support of this motion is made part of this motion by reference herein.

APPENDIX – G MEMORANDUM BRIEF IN SUPPORT OF MOTION FOR LEAVE TO AMEND 28 U.S.C. § 2254 HABEAS CORPUS PETITION:

MEMORANDUM BRIEF IN SUPPORT OF MOTION FOR LEAVE TO AMEND 28 U.S.C. § 2254 HABEAS CORPUS PETITION:

Title 28, U.S.C. § 2254 provided that Habeas Corpus Application "may be amended or supplemented as provided in the rules of procedure applicable to civil actions." Rule 11 of the Rules governing § 2254 proceedings provided that "the Federal Rules of Civil Procedure, to the extent that they are not inconsistent with these rules, may be applied, when appropriate two petitions filed under these rules." The Advisory Committee noted to Habeas Rule 5 points out, in turn that ("under [habeas] Rule 11 the court is given the discretion to incorporate Federal Rules of Civil Procedure when appropriate, so civil rule 15(a) may be used to allow the petitioner to amend his petition. . ."). See Advisory Note 5 of the Rules governing § 2254 proceeding and Fed.R.Civ.Proc. Rule 15(a), taken together these provisions allow amendment of the petition. . . under liberal standards of civil Rule 15. See Hollida -V- Johnson, 313 U.S. 342, 350 (1941), and Withrow -V- Williams, 113 S.CT. 1745, 1755-56 n.7, (1993) (citing FHCPP proposition that Rule 15 applies in Habeas actions.).

Civil Rule 15(a) gives habeas corpus petitioners like other civil complaints, the right to amend the petition once without leave of the court "at any time before [the state files] a responsive pleading." See e.g., Willis -V- Collins, 989 F.2d 182, 189 (5th Cir. 1993). After the petitioner files one free answer amendment or the respondent submits an answer or other responsive pleading, Civil Rule 15 permits amendment "by leave of court or by written consent of the adverse party." See Withrow -V- Williams, 113 S.CT. 1745, 1755-56 (1993). leave to a man shall be freely given when justice so requires. See e.g., Sanders -V- United States, 373 U.S. 1, 10 L.ED.2d 148, 83 S.CT. 1068 (1963). An amendment to a § 2254 or § 2255 motion must be filed within the one-year period of limitations set forth under the 1996 AEDPA. See United States -V- Craycraft, 167 F.3d 451, 456 (8th Cir. 1999).

STATEMENT OF THE FACTS HERE

Plead the facts for the amendment petition here

ISSUE

Argument and Authority here

CONCLUSION

Put Conclusion based on amendment to petition

Respectfully submitted,

/s/_____

[Your Name Here]

APPENDIX — H MOTION FOR LEAVE TO AMEND 28 U.S.C. § 2255 MOTION TO VACATE, SET ASIDE OR CORRECT SENTENCE:

MOTION FOR LEAVE TO AMEND 28 U.S.C. § 2255 MOTION TO
VACATE, SET ASIDE OR CORRECT SENTENCE

NOW INTO COURT comes _____, the petitioner, appearing through pro se representation and respectfully moves this Honorable Court to file an Amendment to (his/her) 28 U.S.C. § 2255 Motion to Vacate, Set-Aside or Correct Sentence, pursuant to Federal Rules of Civil Procedure, Rule 15(a). Leave to amend shall be freely given when justice so requires.

A memorandum brief in support of this motion is made part in this motion by reference herein.

Respectfully submitted,

/s/_____

APPENDIX – I MEMORANDUM BRIEF IN SUPPORT OF MOTION FOR LEAVE TO AMEND 28 U.S.C. § 2255 MOTION TO VACATE, SET-ASIDE OR CORRRECT SENTENCE:

MEMORANDUM BRIEF IN SUPPORT OF MOTION FOR LEAVE TO AMEND 28 U.S.C. § 2255 MOTION TO VACATE, SET-ASIDE OR CORRRECT SENTENCE

Title 28, U.S.C. § 2255 PROVIDES THAT Habeas Corpus application "may be amended or supplemented as provided in the Rules of Procedure applicable to civil rights actions." Rule 12 of the Rules governing 28 U.S.C. § 2255 proceedings authorizes the use of the Federal Rules of Civil Procedure to be applied to § 2255 proceedings.

The Federal Rules of Civil Procedure, Rule 15(a) gives habeas corpus petitioners like other civil complaints the right to amend the petition once without leave of the court "at any time before [the government files] a responsive pleading." See e.g., Willis -V- Collins, 989 F.2d 187, 189 (5th Cir. 1993). After the petitioner files one pre answer amendment or the respondent submits an answer or other responsive pleadings, Civil Rule 15 permits amendment "by leave of court or by written consent of the adverse party." See Withrow -V- Williams, 113 S.CT. 1745, 1755-56 (1993). Leave to amend shall be freely given when justice so requires. See e.g., Sanders -V- United States, 373 U.S. 1, 10 L.ED.2d 148, 83 S.CT. 1068 (1963). An amendment to a § 2254 or § 2255 motion must be filed within the one-year period of limitation set forth under the AEDPA. See United States -V- Craycraft, 167 F.3d 451, 456 (8th Cir. 1999).

State all Facts here
Plead the facts for the amended petition here
Issue
Argument and Authorities here
Conclusion
Insert Conclusion based on amendment to Petition here.
Respectfully submitted,
/s/_____
[Your Name Here]

APPENDIX – J FEDERAL RULE OF CIVIL PROCEDURE 60:

Rule (60) Relief From A Judgment Or Order:

a) The court may correct a clerical mistake or a mistake arising from oversight or omission whenever one is found in a judgment, order, or other part of the record. The court may do so on motion or on its own, with or without notice. But after an appeal has been docketed in the appellate court and while it is pending, such a mistake may be corrected only with the appellate court's leave.

b) On motion and just terms, the court may relieve a party or its legal representative from a final judgment, order, or proceeding for the following reasons:

1) Mistake, in advertance, mistake, or excusable neglect;

2) newly discovered evidence that, with reasonable diligence, could not have been discovered in time to move for a new trial under Rule 59(b);

3) fraud (whether previously called intrinsic or extrinsic), misrepresentation, or misconduct by an opposing party;

4) the judgment is void;

5) the judgment has been satisfied, released, or discharged; it is based on an earlier judgment that has been reversed or vacated or applying it prospectively is no longer equitable; Or

6) any other reasons that justifies relief.

c) Timing and Effect of the Motion.

1) A motion under Rule 60(b) must be made within a reasonable time and for reasons (1), (2), and (3) no more than a year after the entry of the judgment or order or the date of the proceeding.

2) The motion does not affect the judgments finality or suspend its operation.

d) This rule does not limit a court's power to:

1) entertain an independent action to relieve a party from a judgment, order, or proceedings;

2) grant relief under 28 U.S.C § 1655 to a defendant who was not personally notified of the action; Or

3) set aside a judgment for fraud on the court.

e) The following are abolished: bills of review, bills in the nature of bills of review, and writs of Coram nobis, coram vobis, and audit querela.

APPENDIX – K FEDERAL RULES OF APPELLATE PROCEDURE:

APPLICABLE TO RULES 22 & 23
PURSUANT TO RULE 22 HABEAS CORPUS & SECCTION 2255
PROCEEDINGS:

a) An application for a writ of habeas corpus must be made to the appropriate District Court. If made to a Circuit Judge, the application must be transferred to the appropriate District Court. If a District Court denies an application made or transferred to it, renewal of the application before a Circuit Judge is not permitted. The applicant may, under 28 U.S.C. § 2253, appeal to the Court of Appeals from the district court's order denying the application.

b) Certificate of Appealability:

1) In a habeas corpus proceeding in which the detention complained of rises from process issued by a state court, or in a 28 U.S.C. § 2255 proceeding, the applicant cannot take an appeal unless a circuit justice or a circuit District Judge issues a certificate of appealability under 28 U.S.C. § 2253(c). If an applicant files a notice of appeal, the District Judge who rendered the judgment must either issue a certificate of appealability or state why a certificate should not issue. The District Court must send the certificate or statement to the Court of Appeals with the notice of appeal and the file of the District Court proceedings. If the District Judge has decided the certificate, the applicant may request a Circuit Judge to issue the certificate.

2) A request addressed to the Court of Appeals may be considered by a Circuit Judge or judges, as the court prescribes. If no express request for a certificate is filed, the notice of appeal constitutes a request addressed to the judges of the Court of Appeals.

3) A certificate of appealability is not required when a state or its representative or the United States or its representative appeals.

RULE 23 CUSTODY OR RELEASE OF A PRISONER IN A HABEAS CORPUS PROCEEDING:

a) Transfer of Custody Pending Review. Pending review of a decision in a habeas corpus proceeding commenced before court. Justice, or judge of the United states for the release of a prisoner, the person having custody of the prisoner must not transfer custody to another unless a transfer is directed in accordance with this rule. When, upon application, a custodian shows the need for a transfer, the Court, Justice or judge rendering the decision under review may authorize the transfer and substitute the success custodian as a party.

b) Detention or Release Pending Review of Decision Not to Release. While a decision not to release a prisoner is under review, the court or judge rendering the decision, or the Court of Appeals, or the Supreme Court, or a judge or justice of either court, may order that the prisoner be:

1) detained in the custody from which releases is sought;
2) detained in other appropriate custody;
3) released on personal recognizance, with or without surety.

c) Release Pending Review of Decision Ordering Release. While a decision ordering the release of a prisoner is under review, the prisoner must unless the court or judge rendering the decisions, or the Court of Appeals, or the Supreme Court or a judge or justice of either court orders otherwise – be released on personal recognizance, with or without surety.

d) Modification of the Initial Order on Custody. An initial order governing the prisoner's custody or release, including any recognizance or surety, continues in effect pending review unless for special reasons showing to the Court of Appeals or to a judge or justice of either court, the order is modified or an independent order regarding custody, release, or surety is issued.

APPENDIX – L RULES GOVERNING SECTION 2255 PROCEEDINGS FOR THE UNTED STATES DISTRICT COURTS:

<u>RULE – 1</u>:

These rules governed a motion filed in a United States District court under 28 U.S.C. § 2255 by:

a) a person in custody under a judgment of that court who seeks a determination that:

the judgment violates the constitution or laws of the United States;

1) the court lacked jurisdiction to enter the judgment;

2) the sentence exceeded the maximum allowed by law; Or

3) the judgment or sentence is otherwise subject to collateral review; And

b) a person in custody under a judgment of a state court or another federal court, and subject to further custody under judgment of the District Court, who seeks a determination that:

1) future custody under a judgment of the District Court would violate the constitution or laws of the United States;

2) the District Court lacked jurisdiction to enter the judgment;

3) the district court's sentence exceeded the maximum allowed by law; or

4) the district court's judgment or sentence is otherwise subject to collateral review.

<u>RULE – 2 – THE MOTION</u>:

a) Applying for Relief. The application must be in the form of a motion to vacate, set aside, or correct the sentence.

b) Form. The motion must:

1) specify all the grounds for relief available to the moving party;

2) state the facts supporting each ground;

3) state the relief requested;

4) be printed, typewritten, or legibly handwritten; and

5) Be signed under penalty of perjury by the movant or by a person authorized to sign it for the movant.

c) Standard Form. The motion must substantially follow either the form appended to these rules, or a form prescribed by a local District Court rule. The clerk must make forms available to moving parties without charge.

d)   Separate Motions for separate judgments. A moving party who seeks relief from more than one judgment must file a separate motion covering each judgment.

RULE – 3 – FILING THE MOTION/INMATE FILING:

a)   Where to file, and copies. An original and two copies of the motion must be filed with the clerk of the District Court.

b)   Filing and service of the motion. The clerk must file the motion and enter it on the criminal docket of the case in which the challenged judgment was entered. The clerk must then deliver or serve a copy of the motion on the United States Attorney in that district, together with a notice of its filing.

c)   Time to file the motion. The time for filing a motion is governed by 28 U.S.C. § 2255, paragraph 6.

d)   A paper filed by an inmate confined in an institution is timely if deposited in the institutions internal mailing system on or before the last day of filing. If an institution has a system designed for legal mail, the inmate must use that system to receive the benefit of the rule. Timely filing may be shown by a declaration in compliance with 28 U.S.C. § 1746 or by a notarized statement, either of which must set forth the date of deposit and state that first class postage has been prepaid.

RULE – 4 – PRELIMINARY REVIEW:

a)   The clerk must promptly forward the motion to the judge who conducted the trial and imposed sentence or, if the judge who imposed the sentence was not the trial judge, the motion shall be forwarded to the judge who conducted the proceedings being challenged if the appropriate judge is not available, the clerk must forward the motion to a judge under the court's assignment procedure.

b)   The judge who receives the motion must promptly examine it. If it plainly appears from the motion, any attached exhibits, and the record of prior procedures that the moving party is not entitled to relief, the judge must dismiss the motion and direct the clerk to notify the moving party. If the motion is not dismissed, the judge must order the United States Attorney to file an answer, motion, or other response within a fixed time, or to take other action the judge may order.

RULE – 5 – THE ANSWER AND THE REPLY:

a)   The respondent is not required to answer the motion unless a judge so orders.

b)   The answer must address the allegations in the motion. In addition, it must state whether the moving party has used any other federal remedies, including and prior post-conviction motions under these rules or any previous rules, and whether the moving party received an evidentiary hearing.

c) If the answer refers to briefs or transcripts of the prior proceedings that are not available in the courts records, the judge must order the government to furnish them within a reasonable time that will not unduly delay the proceedings.

d) The moving party may submit a reply to the respondents answer or other pleading within a time fixed by the judge.

RULE – 6 – DISCOVERY:

a) A judge may, for good cause, authorize a party to conduct discovery under the Federal Rules of Criminal Procedure or Civil Procedure, or in accordance with the practices and principles of law. If necessary for effective discovery, the judge must appoint an attorney for a moving party who qualifies to have counsel appointed under 18 U.S.C. § 3006A.

b) A party requesting discovery must provide reasons for the request. The request must also include any proposed interrogatories and requests for admission and must specify any requested documents.

c) If the government is granted leave to take a deposition, the judge may require the government to pay the travel expenses, subsistence expenses, and fees of the moving parties attorney to attend the deposition.

RULE – 7 – EXPANDING THE RECORD:

a) If the motion is not dismissed, the judge may direct the parties to expand the record by submitting, additional materials relating to the motion. The judge may require that the materials be authenticated.

b) The materials that may be required include letters predating the filing of the motion, documents, exhibits, and answers under oath to written interrogatories propounded by the judge. Affidavits also may be submitted and considered as part of the record.

c) The judge must give the party against whom the additional materials are offered an opportunity to admit or deny their correctness.

RULE – 8 – EVIDENTIARY HEARING:

a) If the motion is not dismissed, the judge must review the answer in any transcripts and records of prior proceedings, and any material submitted under Rule 7 to determine whether an evidentiary hearing is warranted.

b) A judge may, under 28 U.S.C. § 636(b), refer the motion to a Magistrate Judge to conduct hearings and to file proposed findings of fact and recommendations for deposition. When they are filed, the clerk must promptly serve copies of the proposed findings and recommendations on all parties. Within 14 days after being served a party may file objections as provided by local court rule. The judge must determine de Novo any proposed finding or recommendation to which objection is made. The judge may accept, reject, or modify any proposed findings or recommendation.

c)   If an evidentiary hearing is warranted, the judge must appoint an attorney to represent a moving party who qualifies to have counsel appointed under 18 U.S.C. § 3006A. The judge must conduct the hearing as soon as practicable after giving the attorney's adequate time to investigate and prepare. These rules do not limit the appointment of counsel under § 3006A at any stage of the proceeding.

d)   Federal Rules of Criminal Procedure 26.2(a)-(d) and (f) applies at a hearing under this rule. If a party does not comply with a Rule 26.2(a) order to produce a witness statement, the court must not consider that witnesses' testimony.

RULE – 9 – SECOND OR SUCCESSIVE MOTIONS:

Before, presenting a second or successive motion, the moving party must obtain an order from the appropriate Court of Appeals authorizing the District Court to consider the motion, as required by 28 U.S.C. § 2255, paragraph 8.

RULE – 10 – POWERS OF A MAGISTRATE JUDGE:

A Magistrate Judge may perform the duties of a District Judge under these rules, as authorized by 28 U.S.C. § 636.

RULE – 11 – CERTIFICATE OF APPEALIBILITY:

a)   The District Court must issue or deny a certificate of appealability when it enters the final order adverse to the applicant. Before entering the final order, the court may direct the parties to submit arguments on whether a certificate should issue. If the court issues a certificate, the court must state the specific issue or issues that satisfy the showing required by 28 U.S.C. § 2255(c)(2). If the court denies a certificate, a party may not appeal the denial but may seek a certificate from the Court of Appeals under Federal Rule of Appellate Procedure 22. A motion to reconsider a denial does not extend the time to appeal.

b)   Federal Rule of Appellate Procedure 4(a) Governs the time to appeal an order entered under these Rules. A timely notice of appeal must be filed even if the District Court issues a certificate of appealability. These rules do not extend the time to appeal the original judgment of conviction.

RULE – 12 – APPLICABILITY OF THE FEDERAL RULE OF CIVIL PROCEDURE AND THE FEDERAL RULES OF CRIMINAL PROCEDURE:

The Federal Rules of Civil Procedure and the Federal Rules of Criminal Procedure, to the extent that they are not inconsistent with any statutory provisions or these rules, may be applied to a proceeding under these rules.

APPENDIX – M FEDERAL HABEAS STATUTES:

<u>28 U.S.C. § 2241 – POWER TO GRANT WRIT</u>:

a) Writs of habeas corpus may be granted by the Supreme Court, any justice thereof, the District Court in any Circuit Judge within their respective jurisdictions. The order of a Circuit Judge shall be entered in the records of the District Court of the district wherein the restraint complained of is had.

b) The Supreme Court, any justice thereof, and any Circuit Judge may decline to entertain an application for a writ of habeas corpus and may transfer the application for hearing and determination to the District Court having jurisdiction to entertain it.

c) The writ of habeas corpus shall not extend to a prisoner unless:

1) he is in the custody under or by color of the authority of the United states or is committed for trial before some court thereof; Or

2) he is in custody for an act done or admitted in pursuance of an act of Congress, or an order, process, judgment or decree of a court or judge of the United states; Or

3) he is in custody in violation of the constitution or laws or treaties of the United states; Or

4) he being a citizen of a foreign state and domiciled there in is in custody for an act done or omitted under any alleged right, title authority, privilege, protection, or exemption claimed under the Commission, order or sanction of any foreign state, or under color thereof, the validity and effect of which depend upon the law of nations; or

5) It is necessary to bring him into court to testify or for trial.

d) Where an application for a writ of habeas corpus is made by a person in custody under the judgment and sentence of a State court of a State which contains two or more federal judge judicial districts, the application may be filed in the District Court where in such person is in custody or in the District Court for the district within which the state court was held which convicted and sentenced him and each of such district courts shall have concurrent jurisdiction to entertain the application. The District Court for the district wherein such application is filed in the exercise of its discretion and in furtherance of justice may transfer the application to the other District Court for hearing and determination.

e)(1) No court, justice, or judge shall have jurisdiction to hear or consider an application for a writ of habeas corpus filed by or on behalf of alien detained by the United States who has been determined by the United States to have been properly detained as an enemy combatant or is awaiting such determination.

(2) Except as provided in paragraph (2) and (3) of section 1005(e) of the Detainee Treatment Act of 2005 (10 U.S.C. 801 note), no court, justice, or judge shall have jurisdiction to hear or consider any other action against the United States or its agents relating to any aspect of the detention, transfer, treatment, trial, or condition of confinement of an alien who is or was detained by the United States and has been determined by the United States to have been properly detained as an enemy combatant or is awaiting such determination.

28 U.S.C. § 2242 – APPLICATION:

Application for a writ of habeas corpus shall be in writing signed and verified by the person for whose relief it is intended or by someone acting on his behalf. It shall allege the facts concerning the applicant's commitment or detention, the name of the person who has custody over him and by virtue of what claim or authority, if known.

It may be amended or supplemented as provided in the rules of procedure applicable to civil actions.

If addressed to the Supreme Court, a justice thereof or a Circuit Judge it shall state the reasons for not making application to the District Court of the district in which the applicant is held.

28 U.S.C. § 2243 – ISSUANCE OF WRIT; RETURN; HEARING; DECISION:

A court, justice, or judge entertaining an application for a writ of habeas corpus shall for with word the writ or issue an order directing the respondent to show cause why the writ should not be granted, unless it appears from the application that the applicant or person detained is not entitled thereto.

The writ, or order to show cause, shall be directed to the person having custody of the person detained. It shall be returned within three days unless for good cause additional time, not exceeding twenty days, is allowed.

The person to whom the writ or order is directed shall make a return certifying the true cause of the detention. When the writ or order is returned a day shall be set for the hearing, not more than five days after the return unless for good cause additional time is aloud.

Unless the application for writ and the return present only issues of law, the person to whom the writ is directed shall be required to produce, at the hearing, the body of the person detained.

The applicant or the person detained, may under oath, deny any of the facts set forth in the return or allege any other material facts.

The return and all suggestions made against it may be amended, by leave of the court, before or after being filed.

The court shall summarily hear and determine the facts and dispose of the matter as law and justice require.

28 U.S.C. § 2244 – FINALITY OF DETERMINATION:

a)   No circuit or District Judge will be required to entertain an application for a writ of habeas corpus to inquire into the detention of a person pursuant to a judgment of a court of the United States if it appears that the legality of such detention has been determined by a judge or court of the United States on a prior application for a writ of habeas corpus, except as provided in section.

b)   (1) A claim presented in a second or successive habeas corpus application under section 2254 that was presented in a prior application shall be dismissed.

(2) A claim presented in a second or successive habeas corpus application under section 2254 that was not presented in a prior application shall be dismissed unless;

A.   the application shows that the claim relies on a new rule of constitutional law, made retroactive to cases on collateral review by the Supreme Court, that was previously unavailable; Or

B.   (i) the factual predicate for the claim could not have been discovered through the exercise of due diligence; And

(ii) the facts underlying the claim, if proven and in light of the evidence as a whole, would be sufficient to establish by clear and convincing evidence that, but for constitutional error, no reasonable factfinder would have found the applicant guilty of the underlying offense.

(3) (A) Before a second or successive application permitted by this section is filed in the District Court, the applicant shall move in the appropriate Court of Appeals for an order authorizing the District Court to consider the application.

(B) A motion in the Court of Appeals for an order authorizing the District Court to consider a second successive application shall be determined by a three-judge panel of the Court of Appeals.

(C) The Court of Appeals may authorize the filing of a second or successive application only if it determines that the application makes a prima facie showing that the application satisfies the requirement of this subsection.

(D) The Court of Appeals shall grant or deny the authorization to file a second or successive application not later than 30 days after of filing the motion.

(E) The grant or denial of an authorize application by a Court of Appeals to file a second or successive application shall not be appealable and shall not be the subject of a petition for rehearing or for a writ of certiorari.

(4) A District Court shall dismiss any claim presented in a second or successive application that the Court of Appeals has not authorized to be filed unless the applicant shows that the claim satisfies the requirements of this section.

(C) In a habeas corpus proceeding brought on behalf of a person in custody pursuant to the judgment of a state court, a prior judgment of the Supreme Court of the United States on an appeal or review by a writ of certiorari at the instance of the prisoner of the decision of such state court, shall be conclusive as to all issues of facts or law with respect to in a certain denial of a Federal right which constitutes ground for discharge in a habeas corpus proceeding, actually advocated by the Supreme Court therein, unless the applicant for writ of habeas corpus shall plead and the court shall find the existence of a material and controlling fact which did not appear in the record of the proceeding in the Supreme Court and the court shall further find that the applicant for the writ of habeas corpus could have caused such fact to appear in such record by the exercise of reasonable diligence.

(d)(1) a one-year period of limitation shall apply to an application for a writ of habeas corpus by a person in custody pursuant to the judgment of a state court. The limitation period shall run from the latest of:

A. the date on which the judgment became final by the conclusion of direct review or the expiration of the time for seeking such review;

B. The date on which the impediment to filing an application created by state action in violation of the Constitution or laws of the United States is removed, if the applicant was prevented from filing by such state action;

C. The date on which the constitutional right asserted was initially recognized by the Supreme Court, if the right has been newly recognized by the Supreme Court and made retroactively applicable to cases on collateral review; or

D. the date on which the factual predicate of the claim or claims presented could have been discovered through the exercise of due diligence.

(2) The time during which a properly filed application for State post-conviction or other collateral review with respect to the pertinent judgment or claim is pending shall not be counted towards any period of limitation under this subsection.

<u>28 U.S.C. § 2254 – CERTIFICATE OF TRIAL JUDGE ADMISSIBLE IN EVIDENCE</u>:

On the hearing of an application for a writ of habeas corpus to inquire into the legality of the detention of a person pursuant to a judgment the certification of the judge who presided at the trial resulting in the judgment, setting forth the facts occurring at the trial, shall be admissible in evidence. Copies of the certificate shall be filed with the court in which the application is pending and in the court in which the trial took place.

<u>28 U.S.C. § 2246 – EVIDENCE; DEPOSITION; AFFIDAVITS</u>:

An application for a writ of habeas corpus, evidence may be taken orally or by deposition, or, in the discretion of the judge, by affidavit. If affidavits are admitted and party shall have the right to profound written interrogatories to the affiants, or to file answering affidavits.

<u>28 U.S.C. § 2247 – DOCUMENTARY EVIDENCE</u>:

An application for a writ of habeas corpus documentary evidence, transcripts of proceedings upon arraignment, play in sentence and a transcript of the oral testimony introduced on any previous similar application by or on behalf of the same petitioner, shall be admissible in evidence.

<u>28 U.S.C. § 2248 – RETURN OR ANSWER: CONSLUSIVENESS</u>:

The allegations of a return to the writ of habeas corpus or of an answer to in order to show cause in a habeas corpus proceeding, if not traverse, shall be accepted as true except to the extent that the judge finds from the evidence that they are not true.

<u>28 U.S.C. § 2249 – CERTIFIED COPIES OF INDICTMENT, PLEA AND JUDGEMENT, DUTY OF RESPONDEND</u>:

An application for a writ of habeas corpus to inquire into detention of any person pursuant to a judgment of a court of the United states, the respondent shall promptly file with the court certified copies of the indictment, plea of petitioner and the judgment, or such of them as may be material to the questions raised, if the petitioner fails to attach them to his petition, and same shall be attached to the return to the writ, or to the answer to the order to show cause.

<u>28 U.S.C. § 2250 – INDIGENT PETITIONER ENTITLED TO DOCUMENTS WITHOUT COST</u>:

If on any application for a writ of habeas corpus an order has been made permitting the petitioner to prosecute the application in forma pauperis, the clerk of any court of the United States shall furnish to the petitioner without cost certified copies of such documents or parts of the record on file in this office as may be required by order of the judge before who the application is pending.

<u>28 U.S.C. § 2251 – STAY OF STATE COURT PROCEEDINGS</u>:

a) [In general] -----

1)   A justice or judge of the United States before whom a habeas corpus proceeding is pending, may, before final judgment or after final judgment of discharge, or pending appeal, stay any proceeding against the person detained in any

State Court or order under the authority of any State or any matter involved in the habeas corpus proceeding.

2) For purposes of this section a habeas corpus proceeding is not pending until the application is filed.

3) If a State prisoner sentence to death applies for appointment of counsel pursuant to section 3599(a)(2) of Title 18 any court that would have jurisdiction to entertain a habeas corpus application regarding that sentence, that court may stay execution of the sentence of death, but such stay shall terminate not later than 90 days after council is withdrawn or denied.

b) After the granting of such stay, any such proceeding in any State court or by or under the authority of any State shall be void. If no habeas corpus proceedings or appeal were pending.

28 U.S.C. § 2252 – NOTICE:

Prior to the hearing of the habeas corpus proceeding on behalf of a person in custody of State officers or by virtue of State laws notice shall be served on the attorney general or other appropriate officer of such State as the justice or judge at the time of issuing the writ shall direct.

28 U.S.C. § 2253 – APPEAL:

a)   In a habeas corpus proceeding under section 2255 before a District Judge, the final order shall be subject to review, on appeal, by the Court of Appeals for the circuit in which the proceeding is held.

b)   There shall be no right of appeal from a final order in a proceeding to test the validity of a warrant to remove to another district or place for commitment or trial, fora person charged with a criminal offense against the United States, or to test the validity of such person's detention pending removal proceedings.

c)   (1) Unless a Circuit justice or judge issues a certificate of appealability, and appeal may not be taken to the Court of Appeals:

A. the final order in the habeas corpus proceeding in which the detention complained of arises out of process issued by a state court;

B. the final order in a proceeding under section 2255.

(2) a certificate of appealability may issue under paragraph (1) only if the applicant has made a substantial showing of the denial of a constitutional right.

(3) The certificate of appealability under paragraph (1) shall indicate which specific issue or issues satisfy the showing required by paragraph (2).

28 U.S.C. § 2254 – STATE CUSTODY; REMEIDIES IN FEDERAL COURT:

a)   The Supreme Court, a justice thereof, a Circuit Judge, or a District Court shall entertain an application for a writ of habeas corpus on behalf of a person in custody pursuant to the judgment of a state court only on the ground that he is in custody in violation of the constitution or laws or treaties of the United States.

b) (1) An application for a writ of habeas corpus on behalf of a person in custody pursuant to the judgment of a state court shall not be granted unless it appears that:

A. the applicant has exhausted the remedies available in courts of the state; Or

B. (i) there is an absence of available state corrective process; Or

(ii) circumstances exist that renders such process ineffective to protect the rights of the applicant.

(2) An application for a writ of habeas corpus may be denied on the merits notwithstanding the failure of the applicant to exhaust the remedies available in the courts of the State.

(3) A state shall not be deemed to have waived the exhaustion requirements or be estopped from reliance upon the requirement unless the State, through council, expressly waives the requirement.

c) an applicant shall not be deemed to have exhausted the remedies available in the courts of the state, within the meaning of this section, if he has the right under the law on the State to raise, by any available procedure, the question presented;

d) an application for a writ of habeas corpus on behalf of a person in custody pursuant to the judgment of a State Court shall not be granted with respect to any claim that was adjudicated on the merits in State Court proceedings unless the adjudication of the claim:

1) Resulted in any decision that was based on an unreasonable determination to, or involved an unreasonable application of, clearly established federal law, as so determined by the Supreme Court of the United States; Or

2) resulted in a decision that was based on an unreasonable determination of the facts in light of the evidence presented in State court proceeding.

e) (1) In a proceeding instituted by an applicant for a writ of habeas corpus by a person in custody pursuant to the judgment of a state court, in determination of a factual issue made by a state court shall be presumed to be correct. The applicant shall have the burden of rebutting the presumption of correctness by clear and convincing evidence.

(2) If The applicant has failed to develop the basis of a claim in state court proceedings, the court shall not hold an evidentiary hearing on the claim unless the applicant shows that:

A. the claim relies on:

i.   a new rule of constitutional law, made retroactively to cases on collateral review by the Supreme Court, that was previously unavailable; Or

ii.   a factual predicate that have not been previously discovered through the exercise of due diligence and

B.   the facts underlying the claim would be sufficient to establish by clear and convincing evidence that but for constitutional error, no reasonable factfinder would have found the applicant guilty of the underlying offense.

f) If the applicant challenges that sufficiency of the evidence adduced in such state court proceeding to support the state court's determination of a factual issue made therein, the applicant, if able, shall produce that part of the record pertinent to a determination of the sufficiency of the evidence to support such determination. If the applicant, because of indigency or other reasons is unable to produce such part of the record, then the state shall produce such part of the record and the federal court direct the state to do so by order directed to an appropriate state official. If the state cannot provide such pertinent part of the record, then the court shall determine under the existing facts and circumstances that weight should be given to the state courts factual determination.

g) A copy of the official records of the state court, duly certified by the clerk of such work to be a true and correct copy of a finding, judicial opinion, or other reliable written indicia showing such a factual determination by the state court shall be admissible in the federal court proceeding.

h) Except as provided in section 408 of the Controlled Substance Act, in all proceedings brought under this section, and any subsequent proceedings on review, the court may appoint counsel for an applicant who is or becomes financially unable to afford counsel, except as provided by a rule promulgated by the Supreme Court pursuant to statutory authority. Appointment of counsel under this section shall be governed by section 3006A of Title 18.

i.   The ineffectiveness or incompetence of counsel during federal or state collateral post-conviction proceedings shall not be a ground for relief in a proceeding arising under section 2254.

28 U.S.C. § 2255 – FEDERAL CUSTODY; REMEDIES ON MOTION ATTACKING SENTENCE:

a)   A prisoner in custody under sentence of a court established by Act of Congress claiming the right to be upon the ground that the sentence was imposed in violation of the Constitution or laws of the United States, or that the court was without jurisdiction to impose such sentence was in excess of the maximum authorized by law, or is otherwise subject to collateral attack, may move the court which imposed the sentence to vacate, set aside, or correct the sentence.

b)   Unless the motion and the files and records of the case conclusively showed that the prisoner is entitled to no relief, the court shall cause notice thereof to be served upon the United States Attorney, grant a prompt hearing thereon, determine the issues and make findings of fact and conclusions of law with respect thereto. If the court finds that the judgment was rendered without jurisdiction, or that the sentence imposed was not authorized by law or otherwise open to collateral attack, or that there has been such a denial or infringement of the constitutional rights of the prisoner as to render the judgment vulnerable to collateral attack, the court shall vacate and set the judgment aside and shall discharge the prisoner or resentence him or grant a new trial or correct the sentence as may appear appropriate.

c) A court may entertain and determine such motion without requiring the production of the prisoner at the hearing.

d) An appeal may be taken to the Court of Appeals from the order entered on the motion as from a final judgement on application for a writ of habeas corpus.

e) An application for a writ of habeas corpus on behalf of a prisoner who is authorized to apply for relief by motion pursuant to this section, shall not be entertained if it appears that the applicant has failed to apply for relief, by motion, to the court which sentenced him, or that such court has denied him relief, unless it also appears that the remedy by motion is inadequate or ineffective to test the legality of his detention.

f) A one-year period of limitations shall apply to a motion under this section. The limitations period shall run from the latest:

1) the date on which the judgment of conviction becomes final;

2) the date on which the impediment to making a motion created by governmental action in violation of the constitution or laws of the United States is removed, if the movant was prevented from making a motion by such governmental action;

3) the date on which the right asserted was initially recognized by the Supreme Court, if that has been newly recognized by the Supreme Court and made retroactively applicable to cases on collateral review; Or

4) the date on which the facts supporting the claim or claims presented could have been discovered through the exercise of due diligence.

g) except as provided in section 408 of the controlled substance act, in all proceedings brought under this section, and any subsequent proceeding on review, the court may appoint counsel, except as provided by rule promulgated by the Supreme Court pursuant to statutory authority. Appointment of counsel under this section shall be governed by section 3006A of title 18.

h) A second or successive motion must be certified as provided in section 2244 by a panel of the appropriate Court of Appeals to contain:

1) newly discovered evidence that, if proven and viewed in light of the evidence as a whole, would be sufficient to establish by clear and convincing evidence that no reasonable fact finder would have found the movant guilty of the offense; or

2) a new rule of constitutional law, made retroactive to cases on collateral review by the Supreme Court, that was previously unavailable.

APPENDIX – N RULES GOVERNING SECTION 2254 CASES IN THE UNITED STATES DISTRICT COURTS:

<u>RULE – 1 – SCOPE</u>:

a)   Cases involving a petition under 28 U.S.C. § 2254. These rules govern a petition for a writ of habeas corpus in a United States District court under 28 U.S.C. § 2254 by:

1)   a person in custody under a state-court judgment who seeks a determination that the custody violates the Constitution, laws, or treaties of the United States; and

2)   a person in custody under a state-court or federal-court judgment who seeks a determination that future custody under a state judgment would violate the Constitution, laws, or treaties of the United States.

b)   The District Court may apply any or all of these rules to a habeas corpus petition not covered by rule 1(A).

<u>RULE – 2 – THE PETITION</u>:

a)   If the petitioner is currently in custody under a state court judgment, the petition must name as respondent the state officer who has custody.

b)   If the petitioner is not yet in custody but may be subject to future custody under the state-court judgment being contested, the petition must name as respondent both the officer who has current custody and the attorney general of the state where the judgment was entered. The petitioner must ask for relief from the state court judgment being contested.

c)   The petition must:

1)   specify all the grounds for relief available to the petitioners;

2)   state the facts supporting each ground;

3)   state the relief requested;

4)   be printed, typed written, or legibly handwritten; and

5)   be signed under penalty of perjury by the petitioner or by a person authorized to sign it for the petitioner under 28 U.S.C. § 2242.

d)   the petition must substantially follow either the form appended to these rules, or a form prescribed by a local District Court rule. The clerk must make forms available to petitioners without charge.

e)   A petitioner who seeks relief from judgments of more than one state court must file a separate petition covering the judgment or judgments of each court.

<u>RULE – 3 – FILING THE PETITION; INMATE FILING</u>:

a) An original and two copies of the petition must be filed with the clerk and must be accompanied by:

1) the applicable filing fee, or

2) a motion for leave to proceed in forma pauperis, the affidavit required by 28 U.S.C. § 1915, and a certificate from the Warden or other appropriate officer of the place of confinement showing the amount of money or securities the petitioner has in any account in the institution.

b) The clerk must file the petition and enter it on the docket.

c) The time for filing a petition is governed by 28 U.S.C. § 2244(d).

d) A paper filed by an inmate confined in an institution is timely if deposited in the institution's internal mailing system on or before the last day for filing. If an institution has a system design for legal mail, the inmate must use that system to receive the benefit of this rule. Timely filing may be shown by a declaration in compliance with 28 U.S.C. § 1746 or by a notarized statement, either of which must set forth the date of deposit and state that first class postage has been paid.

RULE – 4 – PRELIMINARY REVIEW, SERVING THE PETITION & ORDER:

The clerk must promptly forward the petition to a judge under the court's assignment procedure, and the judge must promptly examine it. If it plainly appears from the petition and any attached exhibits that the petitioner is not entitled to relief in the District Court, the judge must dismiss the petition and direct the clerk to notify the petitioner. If the petition is not dismissed, the judge must order the respondent to file an answer, motion, or other response within a fixed time, or to take other action the judge may order. In every case, the clerk must serve a copy of the petition and any order on the respondent and on the attorney general or other appropriate officer of the state involved.

RULE – 5 – THE ANSWER & THE REPLY:

a) The respondent is not required to answer the petition unless a judge so orders.

b) The answer must address the allegations in the petition. In addition it must state whether any claim in the petition is barred by a failure to exhaust state remedies, a procedural bar, non-retroactivity, or statute of limitations.

c) The answer must also indicate that transcripts (of pretrial, trial, sentence or post-conviction proceedings) are available, when they can be furnished, and what proceedings have been recorded but not transcribed. The respondent must attach to the answer parts of the transcripts that the responded considers. The judge may order that the respondent furnish other parts of existing transcripts or that parts of untranscribed and furnished. If a transcript cannot be obtained, the respondent may submit a narrative summary of the evidence.

d) The respondent must also file with the answer a copy of:

1) any brief that the petitions submitted in an appellate court contesting the conviction or sentence, or contesting an adverse judgment or order in a post-conviction proceeding;

2) and brief that the prosecution submitted in an appellate court relating to the conviction or sentence; and

3) the opinions and dipositive orders of the appellate court relating to the conviction or sentence.

e) The petitioner may submit a reply to the respondent's answer or other pleading within a time fixed by the judge.

RULE – 6 – DISCOVERY:

a) A judge may, for good cause, authorize a party to conduct discovery under the Federal Rules of Civil Procedure and may limit the extent of discovery period if necessary for effective discovery, the judge must appoint an attorney for a petitioner who qualifies to have counsel appointed under 18 U.S.C. § 3006A.

b) A party requesting discovery must provide reasons for the request. The request must also include any proposed interrogatories and requests for admissions, and must specify any requested documents.

c) If the respondent is granted leave to take a deposition, the judge may require the respondent to pay the travel expenses, subsistence expenses, and fees of the petitioner's attorney to attend the deposition.

RULE – 8 – EVIDENTIARY HEARING:

a) If the petition is not dismissed, the judge must review the answer, any transcripts and records of state court proceedings, and any materials submitted under Rule 7 to determine whether an evidentiary hearing is warranted.

b) A judge may, under 28 U.S.C. § 636(b), refer the petition to Magistrate Judge to conduct hearings and to file proposed findings of fact and recommendations for deposition. When they are filed, the clerk must promptly serve copies of the proposed findings and recommendations on all parties. Within 14 days after being served, a party may file objections as provided by local court rules. The judge must determine de Novo any proposed findings or recommendations to which objection is made. The judge may accept, reject, or modify any proposed finding or recommendations.

c) If an evidentiary hearing is warranted, the judge must appoint an attorney to represent a petitioner who qualifies to have counsel appointed under 18 U.S.C. § 3006A. The judge must conduct the hearing as soon as practicable after giving the attorneys adequate time to investigate and prepare. These rules do not limit the appointment of counsel under § 3006A at any stage of the proceeding.

RULE – 9 – SECOND OR SUCCESSIVE PETITIONS:

Before presenting a second or successive petition, the petitioner must obtain an order from the appropriate Court of Appeals authorizing the District Court to consider the petition as required by 28 U.S.C. § 2244(b)(3) and (4).

RULE – 10 – POWERS OF A MAGISTARET JUDGE:

A Magistrate Judge may perform the duties of a District Judge under these rules, as authorized under 28 U.S.C. § 636.

RULE – 11 – CERTIFICATE OF APPEALIBILITY:

a)   The District Court must issue or deny a certificate of appealability when it enters a final order adverse to the applicant. Before entering the final order, the court may direct the parties to submit arguments on whether a certificate should issue. If the court issues a certificate, the court must state the specific issue or issues that satisfy the showing required by 28 U.S.C. § 2253(C)(2). if the court denies a certificate, the parties may not appeal the denial but may seek a certificate from the Court of Appeals under Federal Rule of Appellate Procedure 22. A motion to reconsider a denial does not extend the time to appeal.

b)   Federal Rule of Appellate procedure 4(a) governs the time to appeal an order entered under these rules. A timely notice of appeal must be filed even if the District Court issues a certificate of appealability.

RULE – 12 – APPLICABILITY OF THE FEDERAL RULES OF CIVIL PROCEDURE:

The Federal Rules of Civil Procedure, to the extent that they are not inconsistent with any statutory provisions of these rules, may be applied to a proceeding under these rules.

Table of Authorities

www.ingramcontent.com/pod-product-compliance
Lightning Source LLC
Chambersburg PA
CBHW081240220326
41597CB00023BA/4224